businesspartners

successful
**decision
making**

For further success in all aspects of
business, be sure to read these other
businesspartners books:

Successful Interviews
Successful Coaching & Mentoring
Successful Project Management
Successful Time Management
Success in Dealing with Difficult People
Successful Communication
Successful Negotiating

businesspartners

successful
decision
making

Ken Lawson, M.A., Ed.M.

NEW
HOLLAND

This edition first published in 2009 by New Holland Publishers (UK) Ltd
London • Cape Town • Sydney • Auckland
www.newhollandpublishers.com

Garfield House, 86–88 Edgware Road, London W2 2EA, United Kingdom
80 McKenzie Street, Cape Town 8001, South Africa
Unit 1, 66 Gibbes Street, Chatswood, NSW 2067, Australia
218 Lake Road, Northcote, Auckland, New Zealand

10 8 6 4 2 1 3 5 7 9

A catalogue record for this book is available from the British Library

NOTE: The opinions and advice expressed in this book are intended as a guide only.
The publisher and author accept no responsibility for any loss sustained as a result of
using this book.

ISBN: 978-1-84773-400-6

Printed and bound in Thailand

contents

Introduction

Sometimes, even the thought of choosing a course of action can render you helpless. You fret about the consequences, implications and ripples that any decision – especially the wrong one – is bound to cause. And in organizational life, you are under pressure to get it right. The decisions you make can set in motion forces that can have a profound effect on your company, your staff and your own career.

Why is it that engaging in the act of deciding can seem so much like walking a minefield? Often, because there is more than one 'right' choice to make. The process might be easier if choices were limited to two very different alternatives – water or wine, north or south or good or evil. But in the workplace, choices are typically far less cut and dried and we often face a daunting slate of alternatives that present a numbing range of viable possibilities.

How do you navigate the minefield of decision making responsibly and professionally? You can leave important decisions to others, or you can make them yourself: with the valuable support and assistance of your colleagues. *Successful Decision-making* shows you how to do just that. In these pages, you'll learn how to arrive at decisions deliberately, methodically, and confidently, without bending to pressures, and without ignoring your best instincts.

With clear, easy-to-read text and a quick-view page format, *Successful Decision-making* provides you with a reliable framework for tackling even the most complex choices. The chapters outline a step-by-step approach to decision making that will help you carry out your responsibilities as a manager confidently and effectively. You'll learn about different types and styles of decision making, and why the best decisions begin with a clear definition of the problem.

You'll find guidelines for identifying and setting objectives, a process that is critical to any successful decision making outcome. Then, once you can define the problem and envision your objectives, you can begin to create options and alternatives. You'll learn the benefits of generating different alternatives and gain tips on gathering information that will facilitate the process.

In Chapter 3, you'll learn how to introduce creative thinking to your
decision making and why it's perhaps the most powerful ammunition you'll
need to solve challenging problems. You'll read why you don't need a
creative temperament to leverage creative thinking in your approach to
decisions. Then, you'll find a wealth of creative techniques that you can use
to generate solutions and alternatives: brainstorming, Mind Mapping®,
lateral thinking and others.

Once you've generated options, you can begin to project their outcomes.
You'll read guidelines for predicting scenarios and assessing risks. Then,
you'll learn how to narrow options based on your projection outcomes.
And, you'll understand why it's critical to factor subjectivity and intuition
into your decisions before you commit to any of them.

Then comes the time to finalize your decision and enact it. In the final
chapters, *Successful Decision-making* shows you how to gain necessary
buy-in for your decision, how to announce it and defend it within your
organization, and how to measure its impact and effectiveness.

Perhaps you're facing a decision to introduce a new product or service, expand into new markets, hire or trim staff or relocate your business to a new city. Or perhaps you're wondering how to become more decisive and effective in your role as a manager. Whatever decision you need to make and however complex and thorny it may be, *Successful Decision-making* will provide you with a trusty road map to chart your course of action and give you confidence in following it.

Ken Lawson, M.A., Ed.M.
Career management counsellor and author
Instructor, School of Continuing and Professional Studies
New York University

1

defining the problem

defining the problem

Benefits of effective decision-making

decision-making is the act of making a choice or judgement between two or more alternatives. These are some of the many advantages that effective decision-making can bring to managers and their organizations:

1 ACHIEVE YOUR GOALS
Making smart choices determines how closely and rapidly you are able to achieve your company's objectives. Decisions are essential for the implementation of any action or strategy.

2 ANTICIPATE PROBLEMS
It doesn't matter how well you've planned for any mishaps, business circumstances can change and take you by surprise. Making a decision that takes into account future uncertainties can help to minimize any damage to your ultimate goals.

3 HIGHLIGHT YOUR LEADERSHIP SKILLS
Most people shirk away from making tough choices because it exposes them to others' criticism. Managers have a lot to lose from mediocre decisions. By making bold, carefully considered choices and persuading others to follow them, you can stand out as an effective leader.

4 CREATE NEW OPPORTUNITIES
Decisions often arise from specific problems. Good decision-making can turn these apparent difficulties into new business opportunities by sparking off new ideas that might otherwise have gone unnoticed. The best decision-makers learn to view problems as opportunities to make positive changes.

5 GAIN IN CONFIDENCE
The more often you follow a systematic approach to decision-making, the easier it will become to tackle future decisions that demand courage and clear thinking. Even when the nature of a decision is very different from a previous one, you can still follow a systematic process that should eventually make you confident about tackling the most complex problems.

6 BECOME MORE PROACTIVE
More often than not, decisions are thrust upon managers by external circumstances. Once you've developed a decision-making style, you will become more adept at creating your own set of problems that you must resolve through smart choices. This means you, not others, are taking the initiative.

Types of decision-making

There are three basic types of decision-making facing managers:

1 OPERATIONAL

These decisions tend to be easier to make because they are routine and repetitive. They involve the day-to-day functions of a company that will already have procedures in place to follow, unless it is a start-up or has been taken over by a second company that has a set of completely different operational practices.

EXAMPLES OF PROGRAMMED DECISIONS INCLUDE:

- How to allocate staff responsibilities and work schedules when a member of the team is on holiday.

- How to compensate overtime – with more holiday time or extra pay?

- How to handle customer complaints.

- Who to involve in recruiting new staff.

- How to organize the annual office party.

- How to allocate a budget.

2 STRATEGIC

Issues concerning the medium- and long-term direction of a company are likely to be less straightforward than programmed decisions. The list of options available is going to be longer as the outcome of the decision is less certain. A greater number of people will necessarily be consulted during the decision-making process, creating more need for negotiation.

EXAMPLES OF STRATEGIC DECISIONS INCLUDE:

- Setting sales targets for the next six months.

- Analyzing the pros and cons of introducing a new line of products.

- Appointing a new advertising or marketing company.

- Finding ways of improving efficiency in a certain department.

- Choosing which staff will lose their jobs during a slow business period.

3 EMERGENCY

These decisions are complicated, like strategic choices, but there is the added difficulty that they emerge from a particular crisis and have to be dealt with almost immediately. You can't afford the luxury of long consultations with interested parties, in-depth research and canvassing of opinions. Mostly made by the most senior managers or perhaps the CEO or managing director, these decisions also have to be implemented immediately and there is no time to persuade staff of the appropriateness of the decision, or the wisdom of the intended course of action.

It is vital in such situations that everyone 'buys into' the proposed course of action, whether they accept that it is the best course or not. In such scenarios, doing something is always more advantageous than doing nothing.

EXAMPLES OF URGENT DECISIONS INCLUDE:

■ How to replace a key member of staff who has resigned unexpectedly or had to take a leave of absence brought about through ill health.

■ What action to take when a fault has been discovered in a company product.

■ How to handle adverse publicity relating to the company, any of its officers, its goods or its services.

■ How to respond to the launch of a new competitor.

■ How to deal with a supplier that lets you down, with the result that you miss a deadline.

■ How to deal with wrong-doing inside your company.

■ How to deal with a *force majeure*, such as a fire or flood you cannot control.

Styles of decision-making

Your decision-making style will depend largely on the type of decision you are facing. Often, it will be made up of at least one or more of the following approaches:

1

PROCEDURAL
This involves following a template that has been tried and tested by the company before. Used mainly for smaller, routine decisions, it demands little individual input by the manager. Watch out for overreliance on what has previously worked well. Managers should ask themselves whether circumstances have changed since this arranged procedure was first used.

2

RISK-AVERSE
Particularly established companies that haven't seen a change of management in a long time are prone to using a risk-averse style of decision-making. This can prove limiting and ultimately create uncertainty because it doesn't take into account any new developments in a particular market or industry. A lot of opportunities can be missed by sticking to old methods that haven't been reevaluated.

3 AUTHORITARIAN

Although a top-down approach to decision-making is becoming increasingly outdated, there are still instances when senior managers have to make decisions rapidly without soliciting others' opinions. In today's more open business climate, this approach is more likely to occur at a multinational company where a decision is made at headquarters and then implemented in subsidiaries overseas.

4 SYSTEMATIC

A well-researched and thought-out approach to a problem is the method advocated in the body of this book. A systematic style includes a precise formulation of a problem, clear goals and objectives, thorough research of different options and a detailed evaluation of the solutions on offer, followed finally by an efficient and swift implementation of the decision. This ideal method is most suitable to strategic decisions and to the preemption of problems.

5 INTUITIVE
The use of logic and clearly defined steps of systematic decision-making does not preclude the use of emotion, imagination and intuition or what is sometimes described as having a 'hunch' or 'gut feeling' about something. A feeling that a particular choice is the 'right' one can complement or reaffirm a decision based on fact-based judgement.

6 ADVENTUROUS
Thinking outside the box can often provide an ingenious or a new and fresh approach to a problem. This creative way of thinking can coexist with systematic and intuitive approaches. Bold changes only turn into unnecessary risks if they are taken in isolation, without having carefully weighed the potential pitfalls.

7 DEMOCRATIC

With growing media scrutiny of individual managers and management practices and the increasing obligation for companies to be seen as socially responsible and caring, more companies are likely to try a democratic approach to management, where team members and subsidiaries are at least asked for their opinions through decision forums, or through a recognized system of representation. This approach is more likely to pay dividends when it is applied in long-term, strategic decisions that affect your range of products and services and most of your employees and their work methods; it is not feasible during emergencies when swift, decisive action is called for.

defining the problem

What is the problem?

The first step in a systematic decision-making process is to define the precise nature of the problem. An accurate and considered description of the problem has a much greater chance of finding a set of solutions than a vague, unformulated problem. The following steps can help you to arrive at a sharply stated definition of the problem.

1 ASK PROBING QUESTIONS

If company revenue is down, one conclusion may be that the overall market environment for the company's products or services is suffering a downturn. 'Nobody's got the money to spend on X right now' is the popular opinion circulating in the office. The implication is that you have to bide your time until the market picks up again. But this interpretation may be the product of lazy analysis or a general unwillingness to combat prevailing opinions.

2 REACQUAINT YOURSELF WITH CORE ISSUES
Why is company revenue down? When did revenue start
to fall? Does it coincide with a change in external
circumstances or can it be tracked to a specific policy followed
by the company? Maybe the market is down but some
competitors are still doing well? Has the company failed to
react quickly enough? Are there other products or services
that could be sold to compensate for lessening demand in the
core business? Never assume that the general perception of a
problem is correct.

3 THINK LATERALLY
Once you've asked the question again, play the devil's
advocate and counter the dominant theories held by company
management. Jot down possible alternatives even if some
appear outlandish and are unlikely to provide immediate
solutions. These alternatives may serve to raise new questions
and you will be closer to defining the exact problem you have
to solve. For instance, is the problem in fact that the company
is not being innovative enough?

4 SEEK OPPORTUNITIES
Perhaps after much questioning, you do come to the conclusion that the market is simply saturated with a certain type of service or product line. But your investigations have led you to discover that, although the market is crowded, there is demand elsewhere for other products or services that your company could be providing more cheaply or effectively than your competitors. You might also identify new markets in different territories.

5 BE DYNAMIC
Through your investigations, you have managed to transform the rather passive inquiry of 'How do we operate in a slow market?' to a more dynamic 'What related product line can we expand?' or 'What related service could we start to offer?' The questioning process is generating fresh ideas and calling for possible further action on different fronts.

6

GATHER OPINIONS

After formulating a new question that you think points to the core problem facing your business, try to open up a discussion with key personnel, perhaps in other departments, about their views on the problem. Use your new assumption (or the original interpretation if you've decided that it is correct, after all) as a starting point for debate.

You might also find that other industry professionals agree with your new premise, or that your call for debate encourages others to think and formulate reasons why the company is underperforming in one or more particular areas.

Other people might offer solutions you have not considered; for example, customer services staff may be aware of a problem through talking to your clients that you might be unaware of. IT staff may know of upgrades or new products that are about to come onto the market.

Checklist: Defining the problem

Before spelling out the definition of the problem, check that you've taken all the necessary steps and posed the requisite questions:

1 Have you given yourself ample time to do research? Are you sure you haven't bowed down to pressure to come to a swift decision on what the problem is?

2 Have you consulted a wide cross section of people inside and outside the company? Have you learned how other firms in your field would define and approach the problem?

3 Have you come up with at least two, preferably three, characterizations of the problem so that you know your final definition has considered all possible options?

4 Is the nature of the problem exaggerated? Should the company be focusing on another problem altogether? ☐

5 Have you distanced yourself enough from the company to look at the problem with new eyes? ☐

6 Does the final definition accurately summarize the main problem facing the company or your department? Are you certain it's not too narrowly focused and that it doesn't allow for the definition to be changed in the future? ☐

CHECKLIST

Final steps

Managers can become so concerned about being seen to be making a visible change that they may decide to start taking action even though the best solution – at least in the short term – is to do nothing at all. How can you avoid embarking on a project for the sake of it? Here are some steps to reassure yourself that you are right in pursuing your objectives:

1 WRITE IT DOWN

If you can, write down in one sentence the nature of the problem that you must try to solve. For example, 'Our company has not diversified enough in a slow market.' This is clear and straightforward without being too prescriptive. It calls for rethinking and urges action, but it does not preempt finding a solution.

2 PUT THE PROBLEM INTO CONTEXT

Maybe you've exaggerated the importance of your particular problem? What other concerns face your company? If you can't think of any, ask trusted colleagues about what issues are preventing the company from growing faster. Does your problem still look like the main priority? What would happen if you didn't do anything about it right now? Can you afford to wait?

3 BE FLEXIBLE
Even at this stage, when you've made your first decision (to formulate the problem), don't be afraid to come back and reexamine the problem definition later in the process. Circumstances continue to change, companies, goods and services change, new markets emerge and personnel change. You have to make sure you're not stuck in old perceptions of the problem.

2

setting objectives

Defining long-term aims

Once you've defined your decision, you need to work out the aim of the decision. One of the most common pitfalls made by decision-makers is to avoid spelling out their long-term goals and aspirations. What do you want to accomplish? Why are you making this decision? The reason is that defining objectives takes time and thought and many people feel pressure to make decisions in a hurry.

WHY IS IT IMPORTANT TO DEFINE YOUR OBJECTIVES?

1

TO GAIN FOCUS
You may have decided that your company's problem – as in the example in Chapter 1 – is that it has failed to diversify its products or services. But how do you know this is really important to the future of your company? This can only be established by answering honestly the underlying question: 'Why are you making this decision?' In other words, what are your ultimate goals and objectives in coming to a decision about your immediate problem?

2 TO GET PERSPECTIVE

The need for your company to diversify may involve significant investments that your company may find difficult to afford. Will that mean a lot of personnel will have to be laid off? How will this affect your current and core business? Is your ultimate goal to take your company into new markets or is your urge to diversify just a response to an immediate problem and not, deep down, part of the company's ultimate aim? By stating your long-term goals, you can put the importance of the current problem into perspective.

3 TO JUSTIFY ACTION

You may decide that the ultimate goal of the company is to gain market share and that to raise the company's share there is no better solution than to diversify. By defining this as your goal, you are now in a much better position to persuade others that the course of action you are about to choose is the correct one.

4

TO RETHINK THE PROBLEM DEFINITION
By trying to pin down the objectives of the company, you may realize that your goals are rather different from the company's. The company may be averse to new product lines because they are too risky. It may prefer to sit out the difficult market and, instead, focus on eliminating inefficiencies in its core business. If you discover that your goals are in fact different from the company's goals, you are now in a better position to reformulate your problem.

5

TO COMMUNICATE MORE EFFECTIVELY
Effective communication is vital to your success as a leader. The more succinctly you can pin down your company's objectives, the easier it will be later to explain any unpopular decisions to other colleagues and subordinates. It will be much easier for others to understand the motives for change if you can put forward a clear, logical argument.

6 TO REASSESS PRIORITIES
On a personal level, identifying your objectives and comparing them to the company's goals will help you to see if you have the necessary support to implement future decisions. If the goals of both parties vary dramatically and you can't find a way of reconciling the two, you may decide that you can no longer play a useful role in the company.

7 TO GENERATE MORE SOLUTIONS
The quality and variety of solutions you and your team can conjure up will depend to a great extent on a well-thought-out list of goals. If you spell out only one or two company goals, then you are limiting the way you think of a problem and it will be easy to overlook any other angles or unexpected ways of looking at the original problem. If you are worried about ending up with too many solutions, it's much easier to discard some later on than to create new ones.

Preliminary questions

The following list of questions is aimed at encouraging you to start thinking about your goals – and those of your company.

Some of them are straightforward and descriptive, while others call for a more considered judgement.

1 What is your company's core business?

2 Do you operate in a mature or new market?

3 Are you a big, medium or small business?

4 What are the company's growth targets for this year?

5 What are the company's growth targets in five years' time?

6 Who are the company's main competitors?

7 Is the company over- or underperforming compared with them?

8 What is the company's annual revenue and profits?

9 How much investment can the company make this year?

10 How much investment can the company make over five years?

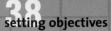

11 How much does the company want to grow?

12 What are your personal goals in the company and in the sector as a whole?

13 Is your company able to fulfil your goals?

14 What is the company's priority in dealing with the immediate problem you are trying to make a decision about?

15 Is the company's priority to minimize losses?

16 Is the company's priority to target new markets?

17 Is the company's priority to keep shareholders or the CEO happy?

18 Does the company have other priorities that you are not up to speed with?

19 What other problems in the company can you identify?

20 Are other colleagues or bosses in agreement?

Obstacles to fine-tuning goals

To further your search for an objective that you may be finding difficult to formulate, here are some common obstacles to defining a goal and suggestions for overcoming them:

NARROW FOCUS

PROBLEM

When you focus on one single, specific aspect of the business, for instance, 'how to lower the cost of TV advertising for product X,' you are in danger of limiting options for action because the objective seems too narrow.

People tend to fall into this trap for several reasons. When looking to make a quick impression on colleagues, it's inevitable to look at short-term gains rather than long-term benefits. The pressure to be seen to be doing something can also be overwhelming, so taking a decision, however poorly thought-out, may be seen as a better option than spending more time looking at the long-term consequences of an issue.

SOLUTION: BROADEN YOUR APPROACH

You need to get to the core of exactly why you need to try to lower the costs of TV ads. The key question is: 'Why is this important?' You may answer: 'Because we are spending too much money on high-profile TV ads'. It's worth asking the same question again: 'Why is that important?' You are being forced to dig deeper still: 'Because we don't seem to be selling more of product X as a result of TV advertising'. Once more, ask the question: 'Why is this important?' 'Because our message is not getting through to our target audience'. Finally, you are getting closer to the company's most basic preoccupation: How to target the company's core market in the most effective manner. While the initial response limited the problem to the high cost of TV ads, the company has now spelled out the problem in a way that provides a wider scope for finding alternative solutions. The new objective hopefully encourages you to look more broadly for solutions. For instance, should the emphasis be on direct mail promotion or on specialized print media?

CROWDED CONCERNS

PROBLEM

When you're trying to juggle too many concerns at once and can't decide how to prioritize, you are unlikely to resolve any of them. This is particularly true when a manager is being pulled in various directions at once. On the one hand, senior management may be pushing to drive down costs and to make some redundancies. Clients meanwhile may be clamouring for speedier service, which means you can't afford to get rid of staff. Finally, employees may be unhappy with certain working conditions that are making them operate less effectively. Which concern should you be dealing with first?

SOLUTION: PRIORITIZE

You have to stand back and decide which of your concerns is the most fundamental to the future of the business. It's useful to jot down the concerns on paper. Imagine the company is a food retailer that has expanded overseas. Although market research and future trends point to high growth in overseas markets, the expansion is undergoing teething problems that are going to incur losses in the short-term. You are also worried that the domestic food market is saturated and there's a need to close down some stores. However, such a move will generate a lot of negative media publicity. On top of this, shareholders are unhappy with returns. You feel you're being pulled in different directions. The easiest option may be to try to please the shareholders and to put a brake on overseas expansion as this will produce the quickest savings. But does this best serve the company's ultimate interests? You have to stop confusing these three concerns with objectives and formulate a separate goal. You may decide that the fundamental company aim is: 'What are the steps we can take to achieve long-term growth?' It is now easier for you to prioritize.

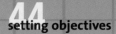

VAGUE FORMULATION

PROBLEM

Insufficient attention to the wording of an objective can create confusion. Take the example of an electrical goods company that has set 'more sales' as its objective for the year. What is meant exactly by 'more sales'? Does the company need to raise the volume of its overall sales? Should it be focusing more on the sale of, for instance, its electric heaters, as an unusually cold winter is boosting demand? Or is it more profitable to concentrate on the high end of the TV set market where margins are currently highest? Is the surge of cheap DVD players from China making it impossible to compete in that particular market? The words 'more sales' fail to specify an approach or a direction on any of these issues.

SOLUTION: SHARPEN YOUR FOCUS

The first step is to expand the phrase 'more sales' into a longer sentence that forces you to clarify the exact intention of the company. For instance, 'more sales' can become: 'We are looking to raise volume sales by 10 percent to achieve revenues of X in the next 12 to 18 months'. Then try turning the statement of intent into a question that urges you to try to think about possible alternatives. Frame the question in a positive way that expresses a desire to improve. For instance: 'How can we best achieve a growth in volume sales?' or 'What are the most effective paths we can take to grow X?'

PERSONAL VALUES VS COMMERCIAL INTERESTS

PROBLEM

It is easy to allow personal objectives to get in the way of making a commercial choice and vice versa. In an ideal world, the company's goals work congruently with your personal objectives. Certainly, the chances of success are far greater if there is harmony between personal and business objectives. But this isn't always the case. Consider the example of the retailer that is expanding overseas. Although the move makes perfect commercial sense, the manager implementing it may find that the necessary overseas travel will mean he won't be able to fulfil one of his personal objectives, which is to spend more time with his family. The manager may unconsciously find business objections to the overseas expansion because it clashes with his own personal ambitions.

SOLUTION: ACKNOWLEDGE YOUR HIERARCHY OF VALUES

More than the previous obstacles mentioned, this scenario demands an honest examination by the manager as to what is fundamentally more important to him at this particular stage: to spend more time with his family or to achieve success in this overseas expansion? He should ask himself several times the question 'Why is this important?'. He may decide that the quest for more family time is not the prime objective and be forced to shift this goal to his list of concerns. To put a blunt point on it, you can't want and have everything you demand. A hard choice has to be made about the dominant objective.

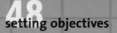

Checklist: Identifying goals

1 Have you formulated your decision question?
Do you have it written down in front of you?

☐

2 Ask yourself why this decision is important to the company.
Jot down a list of possible answers. Don't worry if some of
them seem more trivial than others. This is not the moment
to be critical of your concerns. The important thing is that you
are seeking out all possible options and covering every angle.

☐

3 If you are making a decision in a group or committee, make
sure the other members write their own lists which the
group can collate and refer to later.

☐

Go back to your list and try putting your list of concerns and goals into some order of importance. If you are finding this difficult, try answering the following questions about each concern:

1

■ What effect does this have on the core business? ☐

■ Have other companies in your sector experienced these problems? ☐

■ Are these temporary or long-term problems? ☐

■ If you had to choose the three most important issues, which ones would you choose and why? ☐

CHECKLIST

2 Once you've identified a list of the most important concerns, try asking the question 'Why is this important?' several times.

☐

3 Go back to your concerns and be honest about your own personal objectives. Are you putting your own personal ambitions or preferences before that of the company? Are you being biased?

☐

4 Choose the single most important concern and formulate an objective into a question that encourages action such as 'What steps would we have to take to make sure that X is achieved?' or 'What is the best way to attain X?'

5 Write a list of secondary objectives or concerns that you will have to take into account later on in the decision process.

6 Take a day's break and return to the definition of your objective. Does it still summarize what is most important for the company? Does it invite you to make a decision?

3

generating options
and alternatives

Identifying alternatives

At this stage, you should have a defined problem and a comprehensive grasp of why you need to define the problem. The next crucial step is to find as many possible solutions so that you can make the best choice later in the process. The main advantages of spending time and thought in the search for alternatives are:

1

MORE CHOICE
The final decision can only be as good and far-reaching as the list of alternatives being considered. It's far easier to have at your disposal a wealth of alternatives that you can eliminate at a later stage than to start thinking of new ones from scratch. A broader menu of alternatives also gives others the opportunity to participate in the election of options rather than being presented with only two or three alternatives that you have already edited for them. You may be surprised at how differently a new set of eyes looks at the advantages and disadvantages of a particular option.

2 OUT-OF-THE-BOX SOLUTIONS
It's too easy to rely on tried and tested solutions. Ask yourself if previous methods used by the company to resolve certain problems generated the desired effect. Did people just take the easy way out for short-term gain? Think laterally and creatively to become adept at spotting shortcomings with existing solutions and new opportunities in unexpected sources. The obvious answers are not always the most appropriate in a given situation.

3 ROOM FOR MANOEUVRE

Do you sometimes feel you've been left with little room to manoeuvre? Is it because you've closed off options by not spending enough time researching possible solutions? The earlier you start in the process of finding alternatives, the more angles you'll cover.

4 CHALLENGE THE STATUS QUO

There are invariably two or three alternatives to a problem that you and your competitors can all come up with and these should definitely be included in your list of possible solutions. However, these alternatives tend to be traditional and obvious. Make sure you have at least three more alternatives that challenge well-established assumptions.

5 CONFIDENCE TO CHOOSE
Many decision-makers dither at the last minute about implementing their decision because they are afraid another possible solution may be around the corner. Even though it is wise to remain open to suggestions when making a decision, it also shows maturity and conviction to decide that you are ready to proceed with a choice. This confidence comes from being sure that you have done all your homework.

generating options and alternatives

Identifying relevant questions

The first step in identifying alternatives is to gather as much information around the key decision and objective. To make sure you are gathering the most relevant information and that you have established the correct boundaries, it is useful to check that the following basic questions are addressed at the outset:

1

WHO?
Who is the problem directly affecting? Who should be making the ultimate decision? Who needs to be involved in the decision-making process?

2

WHAT?
What are the main facts of the problem? Are these facts obvious – have they been covered in a company memo or have they emerged from a management consultant report? Or are they more complicated? What needs to be done to find out? What will happen if we don't act? What values does this decision involve for you?

3 WHY?
This is a return to the main objective of the decision. Why does this decision have to be made? Why did the problem spring up in the first place? Why do we have to find a solution?

4 WHERE?
Where exactly is the problem? Is the whole company or a single subsidiary involved? Where does the main responsibility lie?

5 WHEN?
This concerns time frames. Is this an old or new problem? When did the problem originate? By when must a solution be found? How much time do I have time to gather information?

6 HOW?
How did the problem occur? How can we gather the necessary information? How easy is it to access the information? How can I find ways of finding a quick solution?

Gathering information

Now that you've established the initial questions you have to answer, you need to have a strategy for making the maximum use of time available for research. These are tips to follow:

1   SET A TIME FRAME
Try to establish from the start how long you have to collate information. The way you schedule two days of research will be drastically different from month-long research. But be wary – too much time can lead to overanalysis.

2   TIME STRATEGIES
With a very short period, you will be forced to be ruthless about the sources you use and rely more heavily on a couple of trusted people or documents. During a longer period, you'll have the luxury of more time to decide which source best suits your research purposes.

3 ESTABLISH BOUNDARIES
Make sure you are fully aware of the constraints under which you are operating. If there is only a limited budget for a solution, for instance for the purchase of a new computer system, there is no point in spending days trawling through information on new software solutions that might help you solve the problem.

4 ESTABLISH WHO WILL DO THE WORK
The amount of money available for research will also help you decide if you undertake the research personally or whether you outsource it. Establish who is going to do what early on to avoid time-wasting.

5 DOUBLE-CHECK THE BRIEF
Understanding the objective of your inquiries is essential for coming up with the most relevant solutions. You also need to know if you are going to be required to write a report with your findings.

6 FIND OUT FEEDBACK RESOURCES
Will you be passing on the information you have gathered to other personnel to see? If so, should you focus on getting as much information as possible to allow more expert personnel to evaluate what is most relevant? Or will you be evaluating the data yourself? In this case, you will have less time to gather information, because much of your time will be involved in interpreting material.

7 CREATE A TEMPORARY LIBRARY

Build your own library of reports, books, press cuttings and notes. Try and keep an orderly file as you go to avoid confusion when you come to the end of your gathering process and you can't remember where you put that first set of notes. Don't discard any source material.

8 NETWORK

Particularly when you are under time pressure, it's worth calling around all your contacts to check whether they've worked on similar problems in the past. They might be able to direct you to a couple of useful sources or to send you some relevant data.

generating options and alternatives

Sources of information

There are four main sources of information for decision-making:

COMPANY INFORMATION

ADVANTAGES
In most companies, accessing information from the company library should prove the easiest first port of call. You should also, in theory, have quick access to key personnel in other departments, such as the finance department and to company memos and reports.

DISADVANTAGES
Many companies tend to keep every single report and unless there's a particularly efficient librarian, you may find yourself having to sift through a lot of irrelevant information before finding what you want. Colleagues can be an invaluable source of information if they have the time and inclination to help you. You have to rely on their goodwill. Finally, company reports can be biased and deliberately omit any negative information, particularly if they are intended for external use.

CONSULTANTS

ADVANTAGES
A growing number of companies, large and small, use management consultants to offer the kind of objective and expert advice they can't find internally.

DISADVANTAGES
Consultancies have their own procedures to follow when they make audits or visits to companies, especially as they are themselves under increasing pressure to offer a valuable, objective service. You might not have the time that such procedures demand. You also have to be prepared to check up on the eventual conclusions made by consultants. Remember to question even the professionals. Are their values the same as yours?

THE INTERNET

ADVANTAGES

The Internet is an essential source of information, especially as it includes access (a lot of which is still free) to the archives of print publications that might otherwise take a long time to trace. The majority of companies now include information, such as company reports, on the web. Almost all companies and most individuals have direct access to the Internet.

DISADVANTAGES

Just because a lot of information is available doesn't mean it can all be trusted. There is also the tendency to download too much information because it is swift and easy without checking whether the material is relevant. The researcher is then faced with reams of information on a computer that still has to be read and assessed at a later stage.

BUSINESS CONTACTS

ADVANTAGES
Business colleagues working for competitors, analysts and academic experts can often come up with invaluable tips and pointers, especially at the initial stage of information-gathering.

DISADVANTAGES
There's a limit to how long you can rely on informal contacts. People are generally helpful when they are first contacted but time and work pressures mean they can be less willing to cooperate at a later stage.

Using creativity to find alternatives

In the best case scenario, you've had time to complete a thorough research program and to make a list of alternatives available. However, the search for solutions shouldn't end there. The next step is to try and generate as many alternatives as possible. This demands creativity – the ability to approach the problem from a new perspective and in a nonlinear way. It is at this point that many decision-makers seem to face a major barrier, caused by misconceptions about being creative. First, you must dispel these myths, listed below:

SOME MYTHS ABOUT CREATIVE THINKING

1

CREATIVE IDEAS ARE SPONTANEOUS
This is untrue. While creativity involves using your imagination, you have to train your mind to generate new ideas, often by following systematic (i.e., nonspontaneous) tools. Creative ideas come with a flexibility of outlook and an ability to accept change and newness.

2

YOU'RE EITHER CREATIVE OR YOU'RE NOT
Some people may be more disposed to creativity, either because they've actively sought to use their imaginations or because they've been encouraged to. Contrary to what most people believe, creativity is an ability that can be developed over time.

3 YOU HAVE TO BE CRAZY TO BE CREATIVE
In fact, people in so-called creative professions have to spend most of their time perfecting techniques or following laborious and repetitive procedures. Don't be fooled by creative people who appear 'wacky', crazy or out of control.

4 YOU NEVER COME UP WITH ORIGINAL IDEAS
Following convention and learning approved wisdoms by rote are drummed into us at school and even in the workplace. Many people think they can't think of original ideas because they are out of practice.

5 CREATIVITY CAN'T BE TAUGHT
Formal education tends to encourage analytical thinking rather than creativity. We are taught at an early age to follow or create a logical argument, work out a 'correct' answer and eliminate any incorrect paths. However, this focus can undermine another kind of thinking, where we can explore ideas and toy with possibilities. Creativity can be developed using techniques that encourage people to let their mind run free or to complement a logical way of thinking with a different perspective.

Steps to creative thinking

The following is a list of steps aimed at developing your ability to make innovative decisions:

1

BE POSITIVE
Being overly enthusiastic about a new idea is often referred to as 'childlike', which is a negative way of looking at people who come up with bold, surprising ideas. It's far safer to adopt a sceptical attitude to things. Negative people can't be disappointed because they always fear the worst. Try to keep positive by remembering that sceptics are generally scared. If you're stuck in a discussion with negative types, walk away.

2

BE OPEN
Corporations by nature are conservative and operate best when the majority of employees follow a set of rules that have been imposed from above and that remain unchallenged. Examine some of your company's established ways of thinking with an open mind. Don't censure new ideas immediately.

3 TRUST YOUR SUBCONSCIOUS
It's often remarked that the best ideas come to us when we're doing something else. That's because our subconscious is often mulling over a problem long after we've left work. Trust your mind's ability to come up with a solution and write down the bright idea as soon as it appears.

4 SILENCE THE CRITIC
Children learn to mimic their elders early on, silencing new ideas and piling on the 'Yes, but…' responses to apparently outlandish suggestions. Try to silence the critic and allow novel ideas, however off the wall, to settle before you censure them. There is always time for rational questioning at a later stage. Remember to always write down your ideas.

5 TREASURE YOUR THOUGHTS
When you first have an idea, try to keep it to yourself as long as possible so you can really explore its implications on your own. As soon as you start referring to manuals, academic books and other people's opinions (a vital process later on), you stop encouraging other creative ideas to flourish. How many times have you been stopped in your tracks when an idea you thought was brilliant was immediately rubbished by a colleague?

6 SEEK ROLE MODELS
Observing other companies that have taken an unusual approach or launched an innovative product can be a way of motivating others to think out of the box. It also shows that ideas that may appear outlandish, also reap rewards. Think of one company within your sector that has accomplished something unusual and analyze it closely with colleagues. What was special about the campaign, strategy or product?

7 ENCOURAGE IDEAS

There's nothing more discouraging for employees who come up with new suggestions than to have their ideas brushed aside. Allowing people to express themselves, even when privately you think the ideas don't stand up, is essential if you are going to develop creative thinking among your colleagues. If others make snide remarks about any suggestions, let them and others know you won't tolerate mocking behaviour.

Attitudes that block creativity

1 FEAR OF 'PROBLEMS'

Most people tend to react negatively to 'problems', viewing them as events or circumstances that bring failure. As a result, problems are often brushed under the carpet until it is too late to react and an inappropriate response does, indeed, yield failure. Conversely, an exaggerated reaction may encourage swift action without proper thought. By ceasing to see problems as inherently negative, you can learn to turn unexpected challenges into an opportunity to improve things.

2 SOCIAL PRESSURE

A major obstacle to alternative thinking is the powerful pressure to conform and to be ordinary. Invariably, the most successful companies are those that have stuck their neck out and been the most innovative. The rest of the sector then slavishly follows until a brave company once again takes a creative approach. Similarly within companies, the team members who are willing to stand out and face potential ridicule are often the ones who come up with new ways of thinking.

3 'CAN'T DO' ATTITUDE
It's common for people to believe that they are helpless and that they don't possess the knowledge, tools or ability to succeed, so they might as well not try. Poor management structures encourage this kind of helplessness.

4 PREJUDICE
The longer people are in a company or a business sector, the greater the likelihood of garnering a set of preconceived ideas about what is acceptable and what is possible. These preconceptions inhibit people from accepting change and progress.

5 FEAR OF FAILURE
One of the major obstacles to creativity and problem-solving is the fear of failure. The best managers embrace the possibility of failure because it shows that they are at least willing to try their best to accomplish something. They are not afraid to strive for what others think is unachievable and to learn from any possible mistakes.

Eliminating constraints

Once you've been working for a particular company for a certain length of time, you take for granted some of the prevailing attitudes and approaches set out by the corporate culture. In the same way, an entire industry can revolve around perceived notions of how their sector is run, which most members agree with and accept, if only because they have provided a reference and framework for an established period of time. These common assumptions can trap companies and their individuals into a way of thinking. Make a note of some of these constraints detailed below and you will be training yourself to create alternative ways of thinking:

1

IDENTIFY ASSUMPTIONS
Before deregulation, state telecom companies assumed that their role was to provide phone lines and hand sets and that their remit ended there. With the influx of younger, less hierarchical companies, the old monoliths had to start looking at themselves as service providers and to pay more attention to customer service and pricing. But how long did it take them to react because they were locked into antiquated assumptions of their role? Probably a long time. The same is true today of many companies industry-wide. Try to formulate the prevailing assumption of your company. Can you sum it up in a couple of sentences?

2 CHALLENGE ASSUMPTIONS

Now that you've isolated the assumption or a set of assumptions (there may be a subsidiary set of assumptions), analyze the facts and check whether the assumption is valid in today's market or to the particular situation facing the company. It's useful to write a list of reasons why the assumption may still be useful and a second list explaining where the supposition is creating unnecessary constraints.

3 BE AWARE OF CONTEXT

Are the company's core values similar to those of other players in the same sector? Do they all share similar values? Do they differ in any way? Does your company assume other companies operate in the same way?

It can be useful to look at companies in other sectors, particularly if they are in relatively new industries where the constraints of old practices and established assumptions are far less restrictive. Even old-fashioned institutions like banks are having to adopt customer service and marketing tactics that they could afford to ignore in the past.

4 IDENTIFY RIGIDITY
People are averse to change and you must anticipate resistance within the company. Look out for positions that paint the situation in black or white terms. Watch out for phrases like 'We've never done that before', 'Either it's a move towards X or we abandon Y'. Challenge people with rigid positions to explain themselves in detail.

5 QUESTION, QUESTION
Get into the habit of taking nothing for granted. Ask yourself why certain people who are either reluctant to change the status quo or who are in a hurry to push through a decision are adopting a certain stance.

Brainstorming

Brainstorming is one of several valuable techniques that can help you and your colleagues overcome barriers to creative thinking. The idea is literally to create a storm (an unruly web or tangle of ideas) inside your head. The mess inside should free you into thinking beyond the boundaries that are traditionally imposed on us.

There are specific steps in a brainstorming session that should be followed.

1   ORGANIZE A GROUP
An ideal gathering is at least three and up to eight people. Any larger and the meeting becomes unruly and there are too many ideas bandied about. It also becomes inhibiting for the introverts. If the group is larger than eight, make sure you divide into subgroups and compare notes at the end.

2   APPOINT A LEADER
It is important that a group leader oversees the proceedings to make sure that ideas are jotted down and to impose some order and routine. The facilitator is also responsible for explaining the problem or decision that will act as a starting point for the discussion.

3 REQUEST IDEAS
The leader should ask participants in turn to offer up ideas.
Sometimes it is preferable for members to be briefed before
the meeting about the decision so the meeting gets going
immediately. Another school of thought prefers members not
to know beforehand so that responses are spontaneous.

4 AVOID INTERRUPTIONS
The leader must not allow any interruptions or comments on
the ideas as these will stop the free flow of ideas.

5 WRITE IDEAS DOWN
The leader will write down exactly what people say without
putting his or her own interpretation or spin on it. It's a good
idea to write down ideas in separate cards or sheets that can
then be shared among participants.

6 REMAIN OBJECTIVE
At the very least, keep any reactions and opinions to the ideas, however absurd or off the point, strictly to yourself.

7 INVITE DEBATE
The leader should wait to distribute the different cards around until all members have expressed at least one idea or opinion. It's a good idea to get people to read each other's comments so that members don't end up defending their own position. Even at this stage, the convener should keep the flow going by inviting debate on the seemingly craziest of ideas.

8 CLUSTER IDEAS

Once opinions are shared, it should be clear what ideas have been rejected outright by general consensus and which ideas are likely to stimulate further discussion, perhaps at a later date. It is a good idea to try not to disclose the author of the idea in case some people's opinions are coloured by the personality rather than the merit of the stand-alone thought. Try to place some of the opinions into groups to see if a pattern emerges.

9 PREPARE A SHORTLIST

By the end of the session, you should have built a shortlist of four to five ideas or thoughts that best summarize the prevailing ideas in the room. You could take a vote at this stage on the most popular ones and think of having a second vote in a separate meeting to give time for people to digest ideas.

Mind Mapping®

Mind Mapping® is a popular technique used in the business world to question conventional approaches to problems. Like brainstorming, it encourages a nonlinear way of organizing information. Although the technique was formally devised by Tony Buzan in the late 1960s to help students make notes that used only key words and images, concepts similar to Mind Maps® have, in fact, been in use for centuries.

But why use only key words and images? These represent ideas believed by scientists to mirror more accurately the way the right side of the brain, which is linked with the imagination and creativity, functions. Meanwhile, the left side of the brain, which is linked to reasoning, logic and words, is supposedly more receptive to the vertical, logical lists that we are more used to encountering in everyday business life.

GUIDELINES FOR CREATING A MIND MAP®

1
Take a blank piece of paper and start at the centre with an image of the topic under discussion (the problem or decision). The image should represent, as closely as possible, the subject under discussion.

2
Use this central image to create other words or images that spring to mind in connection to the main image. You can use at least three colours that aim to stimulate your visual senses.

3 Each word or image must be alone and sitting on its own line but connected to the central image by a thick line that looks like an arrow or a branch. By adopting your own symbols and designs, you should find it easier to create meaningful relationships between the words or images.

4 Each of the new words and images can, in turn, generate a new set of words that radiate from them, although these will be thinner the further away they radiate from the centre. The lines must be connected, starting from the central image.

5 As in the brainstorming exercise, you should refrain from passing judgement on your map. You will be able to make changes later on.

6 Leave lots of space because often you will come back to the original map and add information or a new set of questions.

7 The idea is that, by the end of the process, your blank piece of paper should be filled with interconnected words and images that have been conjured up by the central theme. You might be surprised how a word in the borders of the paper may assume central importance and provide the key to the central problem. It may even trigger a decision.

Lateral thinking

Lateral thinking is another common technique used in the corporate world to stimulate creative thinking. As the term suggests, lateral thinking challenges conventional (or vertical) thinking by encouraging people to look at an old problem in a new light. One popular technique created by Edward de Bono in the late 1960s involves the so-called Six Thinking Hats, an approach that is explained below.

SIX THINKING HATS

The main premise of this technique is that one of the main issues people face when evaluating a problem is that they take a restrictive view of the situation. For instance, a person following a rational orderly method may be underestimating the power of intuition; a person led by his emotions may be too involved in the problem to take in the tangible facts, while a person who is naturally pessimistic cannot see the opportunities that lie behind the apparent problem.

To avoid these pitfalls, the concept of Six Thinking Hats urges people to look at the problem in several different ways at the same time. Each hat represents a different way of thinking and the idea is that each person involved in the decision-making should try on all the hats during the process. The styles of thinking represented by each coloured hat are explained in pages 89–91.

1 WHITE HAT THINKING

Using a white hat makes you focus on hard facts. The onus is on gathering information and then analyzing the data. If any gaps are missing, it's your responsibility to fill them. You won't accept any sloppy thinking from others.

2 RED HAT THINKING

Wearing the red hat makes you less interested in data, tapping more into gut reaction and emotion. A red hat thinker will try to gauge how other people will react emotionally to a decision. You will also try and empathize with other people's points of view.

3 BLACK HAT THINKING

The wearer of the black hat will point out all the pitfalls of a project. You will tend to be cautious and even defensive, always seeing the ways in which an idea will not work. It's your job to pose awkward questions to the enthusiastic person who can't see how the proposed plan might fail.

4 YELLOW HAT THINKING

When you have a yellow hat on, you are always optimistic, urging the team on even during moments of serious doubt and uncertainty. 'Positive thinking' is your motto.

5 GREEN HAT THINKING
The green hat stands for creativity. You're not interested so much in either the positive or negative aspects of a project. You don't want to pass judgement, either; your main concern should be that the group keeps coming up with new ideas.

6 BLUE HAT THINKING
The person chairing the meeting will be wearing the blue hat as this stands for organizing and controlling the decision-making process. The wearer will try to encourage all participants to speak and make sure there is a good balance of opinions.

generating options and alternatives

Ending the search for options

At some stage, the pursuit of options and alternatives has to come to an end. How do you know when it is time to quit? The following questions should help you decide.

QUESTIONS

1 Do you have a deadline? It sounds obvious, but information-gathering can become obsessive, especially if you think you haven't found the perfect solution. There is hardly ever an ideal answer. In any case, a great solution can have limited impact if there is little time to implement it.

2 Can you gauge from the list of alternatives that assessing their consequences is going to require time and effort? You have to allocate your time across the decision-making process appropriately to give every stage adequate attention.

3 Do you have a comprehensive list of alternatives that you are satisfied covers a range of opinions and assumptions? Or do they all look very similar? If the latter, you may have to push yourself to be more creative.

4 Are you being pushed by another person in the decision-making process to produce results? Are they underestimating the importance of information-gathering? Don't let yourself be pressurized by another person's agenda if you think you haven't completed your task.

5 Are you happy with at least one of your existing alternatives? That may be a good sign, although if you are making a decision in a group, you must produce at least two more valid solutions for others to choose from.

Checklist: Identifying options

1 Have you done your best to identify alternatives? The process of information-gathering and brainstorming is essential. The final decision can only be as good as your list of alternatives.

☐

2 When you start your search, always have the formulation of the basic decision problem and the underlying objective in mind. This will make sure you don't stray from the brief.

☐

3 At the initial stages in particular, put an emphasis on gathering information, rather than processing the facts.

☐

4 Don't be too hasty in your judgements because that may slow you down and also because other people may want to be involved in the analysis of the data.

☐

5 Make sure you've explored all the possible sources of information available. ☐

6 Be aware that the sources – Internet, company reports, other people's opinions – are subject to their own set of criteria and assumptions that might not necessarily concur with your way of looking at things. Stick to as many facts as possible. ☐

7 Have you made sure that you have stuck to the deadline for identifying and creating alternatives? ☐

CHECKLIST

8 Have you made sure that you have stuck to the deadline for identifying and creating alternatives?

9 Apart from gathering information that will lead you to identify alternatives, will you also be looking at ways of creating your own set of alternatives?

10 Are you aware of the underlying assumptions and constraints within the company and the business sector in general that may be limiting the range of options available?

11 Have you been open to the various techniques available to encourage your mind to look at a problem from unorthodox points of view? ☐

12 Have you tried techniques such as brainstorming, Mind Mapping® and lateral thinking with Six Thinking Hats? ☐

13 Have colleagues participated in the creative thinking process, using the techniques listed above? ☐

CHECKLIST

4

projecting outcomes

Predicting consequences

Now that you've got a list of alternatives are you ready to assess how well each satisfies your basic objectives?

Not yet. You still need to refine your list of alternatives by going one step further and projecting these alternatives into the future. What are the possible consequences of following each of the trajectories you've mapped out? Can you make an educated guess at some of the possible outcomes? Only by trying to imagine what could happen in each case can you test the real worth of each option.

It's time, then, to draw up new lists of consequences by methodically working down your existing list of alternatives and describing the outcomes that you expect from each one. Some of these projections will be easier than others, especially if they have been implemented before in your company or by other players in the sector. You should start with these 'safer' alternatives before moving on to the greater uncertainties so that you gain confidence in your ability to project into the future.

WHAT CAN YOU COUNT ON?

Of course, nothing is ever certain in business, as in life. Particularly in today's global market with its 24-hour access to new information, trends come and go at a much faster rate than ever before. But at some point, you have to take a leap of faith and proceed with the assumption that in the best-case scenarios, the consequences of certain actions are indeed foreseeable. In fact, you'll be surprised how many certainties you can count on for any given alternative. The certainties you can work with are those you can calculate – for example, how much investment will be needed to buy machinery for product X or how many sales of Y you will need to break even. These calculations are not guesses – they are carefully worked out.

Test case: Food retailer

Imagine that your company, a food retailer, is considering opening a small outlet in a new property development. How many of the following questions could you plausibly answer? The likelihood is that most of these questions can be answered by the company. Already you can see how you can count on a certain number of certainties when you project alternatives into the future.

1 Has the company opened other small outlets in similar developments before? If so, what was the turnover?

2 Have rival companies launched similar outlets in the area or in similar developments. How did they perform?

3 Are there any food retailers in the vicinity of the development?

4 What is the investment in this small outlet?

5 How many employees will be working at the outlet?

6 Have you done a feasibility study on the project?

7 If not, is there any money available to hire a consultant to carry out a study?

8 Will the opening of this outlet be at the expense of opening in other locations?

9 Where will the company invest if this plan is dropped?

10 How crucial is this opening for the company's growth plans?

11 What are the cost implications of pursuing one option rather than another?

Your organization

How can you do your best to forecast all possible outcomes of a potential decision? Identifying your company's Strengths, Weaknesses, Opportunities and Threats (a popular technique known as SWOT) can help you amass valuable facts that will help you make a credible prediction of future outcomes.

QUESTIONS TO ASK ABOUT YOUR COMPANY

These can also be used on companies that compete with yours.

STRENGTHS

- What advantages does your company have over its major competition?
- What strengths do competitors identify in your company?

- What are your company's biggest selling points?
- Which is the most profitable division in your company? Why is this?

WEAKNESSES

- Where and how is the company underperforming?
- What weaknesses do competitors dwell on?

- What areas are most in need of improvement?
- Which competitors are doing better and why?

OPPORTUNITIES

- What are the areas of strongest growth in the sector?
- Are there any future trends you should be taking advantage of?

- Where are the biggest chances for growth?
- What competitive advantages can you exploit?

THREATS

- What are the biggest obstacles facing you?
- Are there any government regulations or societal changes that are going to affect you?

- What are your competitors doing that you are not?
- Does the company face a shortage of investment capital or resources?

A comprehensive grounding on the core competencies of your company and its standing in its sector can help you come to confident conclusions about future trends and eliminate many uncertainties about a move that appears risky on the surface.

WHAT IS YOUR COMPANY'S ATTITUDE TO NEW IDEAS?

Knowing hard facts about your company's financial and operating history is just a first step in counting up certainties. But what about the slightly less tangible details of how your company responds to new ideas and change? Understanding your corporate culture and core values can also assist you in mapping out the feasibility of your proposed set of alternatives.

These are some of the questions you can ask yourself about your company to identify how acceptable your proposal is:

1 Is your company conformist and traditional, relying on tried and tested methods rather than on bold, fresh initiatives?

2 What is your reputation in the company?

3 Do you think you will be taken seriously or do you have to get other members on-side first?

4 How well do you know the politics of the company? Does your approach have to cater for this?

5 Do you have to pander to certain senior decision-makers who like to feel they have come up with ideas themselves?

6 Which lever at the top of the company may have to be pulled for a proposal to be accepted?

7 How often does the company change its mind on policy issues?

8 Does the company tend to lead a trend or chase competitors?

9 When was the last time the company took a major risk?
Was the outcome successful?

10 Does the company have the right kind of employees to put your proposal into action?

11 How receptive will junior staff members be to the kind of changes you are proposing?

12 If you are given the green light, do you foresee a major battle in implementing the decision?

Predicting scenarios

There are several instances when knowledge about your company's financial situation or its corporate culture is not sufficient to brush away major imponderables about the outcomes of your list of alternatives. This is the point where you have to take some bolder steps to forecast the future.

1

ASK 'WHAT IF' QUESTIONS
Be prepared to map out a response to a worst-case scenario. For instance, if the food retailer goes ahead with the store opening in the new development and there is a six-month delay in the completion of the residential blocks, how will this affect sales? Will you be able to release staff given that there are few customers? How flexible can you be? In this case, you are doing more than forecasting the future, you are already setting up potential contingency plans.

2

WORK BACK FROM THE FUTURE
Like the earlier example, this involves making a proactive decision because you are starting off by imagining your desired outcome and then working backwards to see what steps you would have to take to achieve it.

3 ASSESS SUCCESS

You can also try using 'probability theory' to lower the element of error. You do this by working out the likelihood of an event happening on a scale of 1 (impossible) to 5 (guaranteed) with a 50:50 chance of success at 3. You can then multiply the set of possible investments by these probabilities to gauge which gives you the better figures.

4 SIMULATE THE FUTURE

You can try enacting the future using computer programs to work out complex equations using a range of possible scenarios, both positive and negative. Computer graphics help to illustrate the points to other staff members.

5 HIRE CONSULTANTS

When in-house resources are unable to carry out complicated calculations, you can try consultants with both the know-how and experience.

Risk profiles

Risk profiling is a useful technique that grasps the basic information about the way uncertainty affects your alternatives. There are four key steps:

1 SELECT THE MAIN UNCERTAINTIES
As not all uncertainties can have a major impact on the future, it's useful to identify which of the many uncertainties are important enough to highlight in a list. When you've reviewed them, chose three to five uncertainties. Take one at a time and describe the way they could impinge on the decision. You might continue to eliminate the ones with lower impact from the list. Try to single out the most important uncertainty.

2 SPECIFY OUTCOMES
Following the same sequence as above, try to refine a list of possible outcomes and to describe them. Make sure the chosen outcomes clearly differ from each other, that they include all possible scenarios and that they are clearly defined.

3 GUESS THE ODDS

What are the odds of each outcome being played out? If you find this difficult, use your judgement, refer to any factual information available or ask the relevant specialists. Be as specific as possible by using a percentage or a ratio, not a vague phrase like 'fairly likely' or 'average chance'.

4 DEFINE CONSEQUENCES

With the same care you took to specify an outcome, you should now try to describe neatly and succinctly what the possible consequences of each outcome are.

By the time you've completed the four steps and forced yourself to eliminate peripheral uncertainties and outcomes and isolated the single most important concerns, you should be in a much better position to grade the potential impact of each alternative and make a decision.

Checklist: Projecting outcomes

1 Have you formulated clearly and concisely the consequences of your alternatives?

2 Have you written them down and put them in a list that you can return to and access immediately?

3 How well do the alternatives you have created fit the criteria: the decision problem and the main objective?

4 When you look at your list of consequences, does it help you make up your mind about your main objective and decision problem? If so, the consequences have been clearly defined and will make the process of selection much easier and faster. ☐

5 Have you gathered as much information as possible about your company's financial record and corporate culture? ☐

6 Can you now make an assessment about the company's ability to finance the project? ☐

CHECKLIST

7 How does each alternative fit in with the culture of the company? ☐

8 How does the alternative fit in with the ethos of the senior management? Is it too conservative or will the progressive directors find it too timid? ☐

9 Have you assessed the probability of each possible outcome? ☐

10 Have you grasped the importance of making informed predictions about the future? ☐

11 Are you aware of some of the routines you can follow to help you minimize the impact of uncertainty on your decisions? ☐

12 Have you thought of all the variables and alternatives involved in making predictions? ☐

13 Have you allowed for any margin for error in your forecasting? ☐

CHECKLIST

5

narrowing the options

Cutting down the alternatives

This section covers a range of well-known techniques to help you reduce the long list of alternatives you should now have compiled. It tells you the benefits of each technique and outlines the way to use it. Inevitably, there will be a certain amount of overlap between some of the approaches.

PROS AND CONS

Listing the advantages and disadvantages of each different course of action forms the crux of all the techniques that have been devised for business in the last few decades. Sometimes the pros and cons of each alternative use such different criteria that it is difficult to make a direct comparison. This is where you have to start making value judgements, assigning points to each of the criteria, adding up the totals and choosing the alternative with the highest score.

The techniques outlined use the pros and cons strategy as a basic framework and then provide their own twists and tweaks to the basic premise. Which one should you pick? The method that works best for you depends on the nature of your problem, your personal approach to problem solving and which set of criteria is most important to you and the company at the time. Is cutting costs the main priority or is the company seeking for an innovative project that will reap benefits in the longer term? Is it a strategic or emergency move? Combining different sorts of techniques may work best for you and ensure that you understand all sides of the argument.

narrowing the options
Grid analysis

PURPOSE

When there is no obvious single objective, grid analysis helps you choose between multiple options, when there are many and seemingly conflicting alternatives to consider.

HOW TO USE IT

1 First make a list of all your alternatives and then make a second list with all the factors.

For instance, a corporation is considering opening its first Asian subsidiary. The three alternatives are Malaysia, India and China, which we can refer to as countries A, B and C. The factors under consideration are the cost of acquiring premises (property values), the presence of other companies in the market, the local competition, the tax regime and labour costs.

2 Draw a table, putting the countries in a column down the left edge and important factors across the top.

3 Now you have to decide which of the factors is most important. Use a scoring system of 1–10. If you are finding it difficult to assign values, refer to 'Paired Comparison Analysis' (see pp. 130–133).

4 Work your way across the table, scoring each option but using a different system to the factor list. Try using 0–3, with 0 representing poor and 3 very good. Don't worry if the scores are the same.

5 Multiply each of your factor scores by the value scores. You should now have the correct overall weight in your decision.

GRID ANALYSIS

COUNTRIES	FACTORS	PROPERTY VALUES 6	WESTERN COMPETITION 3	
A		1 (6)	1 (3)	
B		2 (12)	2 (6)	
C		3 (18)	2 (6)	

For instance, C might appear to score high in terms of low property and labour costs and the absence of foreign competition, but it scores low in the tax regime factor. You might decide that the prohibitive tax system minimizes all the other advantages. A might be a more mature market with more competition and higher start-up costs, but its lower taxes makes it a better business option in the longer term.

	LOCAL COMPETITION 4	TAX REGIME 9	LABOUR COSTS 5	TOTAL
	2 (8)	3 (27)	2 (10)	54
	2 (8)	1 (9)	2 (10)	45
	1 (4)	1 (9)	3 (15)	52

Tradeoffs

PURPOSE

■ The tradeoff is a slightly different version of grid analysis. The goal is similar: the acknowledgement that, in some cases, there are several competing objectives and that you have no choice but to make some compromises.

■ Tradeoffs help you focus on the real value of each alternative and how it best serves your original objective.

HOW TO USE IT

1
List all your objectives down the left side of a page and your alternatives along the top to give you an empty matrix. Your objectives may be to initiate an expansion overseas with Asia as the top preference for a launch. The main question is which of the chosen three countries in that area – A, B or C – will achieve the highest yields. You might include two smaller and less-developed countries – D and E – as less attractive options, but ones worth investigating.

2
Work through each objective and evaluate which consequence gets closest to meeting your goal. The rankings help you see immediately which consequence has the most advantages. The best option will score 1, the second-best option 2 and so forth.

At this stage, it may already be easy to see that D and E rank too low and that there are no benefits in taking these options any further. The other three countries are dominant alternatives.

3 Make swaps. This entails writing a list of advantages and disadvantages for each of the three remaining countries. Score each factor using 0–3, with 0 representing poor and 3 very good. For example, B scores high on the corporation's target market because consumer spending has been highest. Property prices however have almost doubled in the last three years. In country C, property prices may be lower but so is consumer spending power. Labour costs also vary dramatically in the three places.

At some point, you can start cancelling out the various pros and cons by making informed swaps. For instance, the cost of travelling from the company head office to A is much higher than to B, but hotel prices are lower, effectively cancelling the flight disadvantages. The cost of travel and hotel in country C is moderate and so, as the combined score is 3 for each country, you can now cancel or eliminate both factors from your decision because they even each other out. You are now able to focus on fewer factors that may take longer to quantify.

TRADEOFFS (FIGURE 1)

OBJECTIVES	A	B	C	D	E
Establish launch pad for Asia	5	4	3	2	1
Generate profits (4% p.a.)	5	3	4	1	2
TOTAL	10	7	7	3	3

TRADEOFFS (FIGURE 2)

ADVANTAGES/ DISADVANTAGES	ALTERNATIVES		
	A	B	C
High consumer spend	2	3	1
Low property prices	2	0	3
Low labour costs	3	1	2
Costs of travel	0	3	2
Costs of hotel	3	0	1
TOTAL	7	4	6

Paired comparison analysis

PURPOSE

- Paired comparison analysis helps you weigh the relative value of different courses of action.

- Unlike other techniques, it should also give you a clearer idea of where your priorities lie.

HOW TO USE IT

1 You begin by listing all your options (in the case of the corporation planning an Asian expansion, list the three possible country launches: A, B and C).

2 Draw up a grid with each option as both a column header and a row.

3 One by one, compare each option (the one in the row with the one in the column) using this grid. You will have to block out cells on the table where you will be comparing an option with itself. These will come on the diagonal running from the top left to the bottom right.

4 For each cell, decide which of the two options is more important. Write down the letter of the more important option in the cell and score the difference in importance from 0 (no impact) to 4 (major impact).

5 Add up the total of all the values for each of the options. A might score 1, B might score 2 and C might score 4. It might be useful to convert these values into a percentage of the total score so that a score of 1 becomes 14 percent, 2 is 29 percent and 4 is 57 percent. Clearly C, with a score of 57 percent, looks like the best option in this analysis.

PAIRED COMPARISON ANALYSIS

COUNTRIES	A	B	C
A	X	B2	A1
B	X	X	C4
C	X	X	X

	TOTAL SCORE		
		A	= 1
		B	= 2
		C	= 4

Decision tree analysis

PURPOSE

- 'Decision trees' help you to choose between several courses of action by providing a structure within which you can map out options and analyze the possible consequences of choosing those options.

- They provide a balanced picture of the benefits and risks linked with each potential option.

HOW TO USE IT

1 On the left-hand side of a blank sheet, write down the decision problem. In this case, it is in which Asian country will a corporation roll out its first branch? Next to it, draw a small square to represent the decision problem.

2 Draw out lines from the box toward the right to represent each alternative. Write a short description of each alternative. Try and keep the lines as far apart as possible to allow you to add other alternatives and to give you room for more notes later on.

3 At the end of the line, now write any clear-cut consequences (for instance, possible market shares achievable in the sector). If the result is that you have to make another decision, draw another square that represents a decision problem. If the outcome is uncertain (there are no other foreign competitors present so it's difficult to gauge how well similar products sell), then draw a small circle that represents an undefined resolution.

4 By the new box, repeat steps two and three. The list of options and decision problems should be fanning out like branches of a tree. You're ready to review the tree diagram.

5 It's time to give the different components different values. Assign a cash value to each possible outcome. Work out which option is worth most to you. Then look at each circle (representing an uncertainty point) and estimate the probability of each outcome.

6 To calculate the value of uncertain outcomes (circles on the diagram), multiply the value of the outcomes by their probability. The total for that node of the tree is the total of these values.

DECISION TREE DIAGRAM

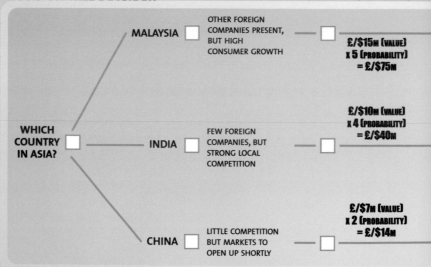

MALAYSIA — OTHER FOREIGN COMPANIES PRESENT, BUT HIGH CONSUMER GROWTH — £/$15M (VALUE) x 5 (PROBABILITY) = £/$75M

WHICH COUNTRY IN ASIA?

INDIA — FEW FOREIGN COMPANIES, BUT STRONG LOCAL COMPETITION — £/$10M (VALUE) x 4 (PROBABILITY) = £/$40M

CHINA — LITTLE COMPETITION BUT MARKETS TO OPEN UP SHORTLY — £/$7M (VALUE) x 2 (PROBABILITY) = £/$14M

7 To evaluate a decision node, write down the cost of each option along each decision line. Then, subtract the cost from the outcome value that you've already calculated. You now have the value that represents the benefit of that decision.

☐ IS THERE ROOM FOR MORE ENTRIES?	—————	YES AND WE HAVE STRONG PRODUCTS	**x3 (PROBABILITY) = £/$225M**
☐ CAN FOREIGNERS BUY LOCAL COMPANIES?	—————	YES, BUT OTHER FOREIGN COMPANIES MAY HAVE THE SAME IDEA	**x3 (PROBABILITY) = £/$120M**
☐ WILL LOCAL MARKETS GROW?	—————	◯ POSSIBLY, NO RELEVANT DATA	**x 0 = ABANDON PROJECT**

Plus/Minus/Implications (PMI)

PURPOSE

■ Like all the other methods, PMI, codified by Edward de Bono (see 'Six Thinking Hats' on pp. 88–91) helps you weigh the pros and cons of a decision, but it goes one step further by making you think of the implications of a decision.

■ PMI is effective for checking whether a decision is likely to improve the situation.

HOW TO USE IT

1 Draw up a table with three columns headed Plus, Minus and Implications.

2 In the column under 'Plus' write down all the positive results of taking the action. In the case of the corporation considering a foray into Asia, this could include using the launch as an entry to the less developed Asian markets, proximity to production lines and low investment costs.

3 Under 'Minus' write down all the negative effects, such as the volatility of the local economy, the lack of information on the sector and high taxes.

4 In the 'Implications' column, write down the implications and possible outcomes of taking the action. These could include establishing a presence in the local market before other foreign competitors move in or allocating too many resources at head office to the expansion during a difficult time in the company's core market.

5 By this stage, it may already be obvious whether or not your plans will work. If you are still unclear, consider each of the implications and assign a positive and negative score. As you are scoring implications (rather than hard facts), it's inevitable that some of the scores will be subjective.

PLUS/MINUS/IMPLICATIONS

PLUS	MINUS	IMPLICATIONS
Launch pad for whole of Asia (+6)	Volatility of local economy (-4)	Positive long-term prospects (+2)
Proximity to production lines (+5)	Lack of information on sector (-3)	Fast access to markets (+2)
Low investment costs (+4)	High taxes (-4)	Taxes may fall to attract investment (0)
TOTAL: 15	-11	+4
		15 - 11 + 4 = 8

narrowing the options

Cost–benefit analysis

PURPOSE

■ Unlike the other techniques that involve some degree of subjectivity in their evaluation, cost–benefit analysis has a more defined goal: letting you know if can you afford this decision, regardless of the other merits of the case.

■ As its name suggests, the technique essentially adds up the value of the benefits of a course of action and subtracts the costs associated with it. In the case of the corporation's decision whether to open a branch in Asia, the concern is only whether the direct benefits (sales figures) will compensate for the investment (red tape, cost of purchasing property and labour costs). It doesn't take into account less quantifiable costs such as the value of having a physical presence in a region that has potential for explosive growth in the future. However, the calculation of the benefits can sometimes be subjective, as benefits are mostly received in the long term, whereas costs are often seen in the short term. These can include payments made at specific times, such as the acquisition of property at the initial stages.

HOW TO USE IT

1 Make a calculation of costs, both single occurrence and ongoing. This will include the cost of the red tape necessary to establish a foreign subsidiary, the price of leasing or buying a property, the money needed to refurbish the property, labour costs and travel and hotel expenses incurred during the preliminary negotiations.

2 A payback period can be slightly more complicated to calculate. You have to specify a period of time, for instance two to three years, which may be the average time it takes for any change in your business to see real returns.

narrowing the options

Pareto analysis

PURPOSE

■ Pareto analysis is a simple but commonly used principle that helps you to identify the most important problem to solve.

■ The idea behind the Pareto principle is that by doing 20 percent of the work you can generate 80 percent of the advantage of doing the entire job. In other words, making a change to just one aspect of your business – assuming it is the correct one – can generate far more benefits than if you make changes to various aspects at once.

HOW TO USE IT

1 List the problems. Assume in this case that the corporation has opened a branch in Asia (China for example) and is now facing unexpected problems with staff performance that are affecting sales. There are three main problems: Staff are not used to offering customer service and only respond to clients when asked; staff have a low understanding of the company products; and a customer survey indicates that there are too few staff.

2 Group the options available. These might be hiring more staff, appointing a new shop manager, planning better training or changing product lines. Give each alternative a score that takes into account the potential benefits (plus points) and the cost involved (negative points).

3 Examine the final scores. The options with the lowest scores can now be discarded. Hiring more staff might look like the most obvious solution, but the cost involved is too high. To appoint a new manager will be time-consuming. According to the customer complaints, the staff's attitude to service (low) was the main problem. Improving staff motivation looks like the option that will resolve the greatest number of issues. This is based on the assumption that tackling one single problem (at least 20 percent of the range of problems) will generate at least 80 percent of the solution.

PARETO ANALYSIS

OPTIONS	BENEFITS/COSTS		
	EFFECTIVENESS	COST	TOTAL
Appoint more staff	+8	-5	3
Appoint new manager	+5	-5	0
Better training	+6	-3	3
Change product line	-1	-10	-11

(Scores out of 10)

Calculating risk

The different variations of the basic pros and cons approaches to making decisions acknowledge an element of uncertainty in their calculations, but they are not aimed at evaluating decisions that involve a higher element of risk. This section explores the role of risk-taking in decision-making.

YOUR ATTITUDE TO RISK

■ For a better understanding of the pros and cons of a decision, you need to understand and acknowledge your tolerance (or lack of it) for risk and to compare your attitude to your company's approach, which may be more risk-averse or, alternatively, more adventurous. Ask yourself whether you generally look at a glass as half full or half empty.

■ Consider the case of the corporation planning an Asian expansion. The optimist will home in on the potential for market growth in the next decade and the importance of being one of the first Western companies to establish a foothold in a more or less virgin sector. The pessimist will focus on the immediate problems: the teething stage, the cultural differences that may affect business practices, the slow acceptance by the market.

NEUTRALIZING YOUR RISK ATTITUDE

To avoid allowing your own prejudices and experiences with risk to colour your decision, consider some of these points:

1 DON'T OVER- OR UNDERCOMPENSATE
Many people tend to underplay the possibilities of success and are especially fearful of failure. It's a human reaction to avoid disappointment. However, if you apply this non-scientific and subjective attitude to all your risk calculations, you are likely to be overcautious. Try to judge how objective you are being in your calculations.

2 DON'T ASSUME
If you haven't properly weighed up the range of alternatives
on offer and assume that the most probable one will occur,
you may be unpleasantly surprised. You need to bear in mind
all possibilities and also calculate how likely they are to
happen. For example, try to look at sales growth not only from
the point of view of your company but also on the basis of
new competitors entering the market or a well-known, local
company venturing into the sector.

3 TAKE OFF ROSE-TINTED GLASSES
The desire for success can also make people blind to many of
the potential pitfalls and lead decision makers to almost
discard any possibilities that defer from the winning outcome.
It's good to think positively, but you have a responsibility to act
in a realistic and pragmatic manner.

4 BE AWARE OF COMPANY ETHOS
Is your company traditionally wary of change and slow to react to market events or does it have a record for innovation and taking bold steps? Are you in tune with the overriding company ethos or out of step? If your views and attitudes do differ, be realistic and be aware that you are operating in a context with limits.

5 BOUNCE OFF IDEAS
It's easy to become so personally involved with a decision and its consequences that you no longer feel able to judge its potential for success or failure. This is particularly the case when you have a lot of your own career development vested in the outcome. Find a trusted colleague, not necessarily in the same company, and have them play devil's advocate. They may be able to spell out the opportunities or dangers you are facing.

Estimating risk: Risk analysis

Estimating a risk may sound like a contradiction in terms. If you could actually calculate the probability of something good or bad happening, it would no longer be a risk. However, there are steps you can take to make sensible evaluations and even to try to control risks.

1 IDENTIFY ORGANIZATIONAL THREATS

The first stage of a risk analysis is to identify the main threats and obstacles. These can take several guises. Consider the example of the corporation planning a foray into Asia:

- **OPERATIONAL:** A fall in sales, problems with distribution, poor customer service.

- **HUMAN:** Resignation of personnel, illness, even death.

- **REPUTATIONAL:** Staff lose faith, reputation in the market affects stocks.

- **FINANCIAL:** A dive in the stock market, a hike in interest rates.

- **PROCEDURAL:** Disagreements between head office and overseas subsidiary.

2   IDENTIFY ENVIRONMENTAL THREATS

■ NATURAL: Freak weather, rivers in city centre flooding, damage to the fabric of buildings.

■ POLITICAL: A change in the tax regime, a backlash against foreign companies.

3   CALCULATE RISK

Make an estimate of the probability of any of these threats actually happening and multiply this by the amount it will cost to correct the problem. In other words, the value (or cost) of the risk is the probability of the event happening multiplied by the cost of righting the event.

4 MANAGE RISK

There are a number of ways of managing risk:

■ **PLAN FOR CONTIGENCIES:** Having accepted that a certain threat may happen (like a new government raising taxes for foreign companies), you can develop a plan to minimize its effects. Consider what the best and worst things that can reasonably happen are. This way, you can estimate whether the potential benefits of the best-case scenario outweigh the worst-case scenario.

■ **USE EXISTING ASSETS:** You may try to minimize risks by making improvements to all the areas that could be under threat. For instance, in the case of operations, there are always active ways of improving customer services, finding a more efficient distribution network or lowering overheads.

5 MORE WAYS TO MANAGE RISK

- **INSURE AGAINST RISK:** Particularly in the case of freak weather but also with financial loans, there is the possibility of insuring some risky elements.

- **DIVERSIFY RISK:** The company can make financial arrangements to spread their investments.

6 REVIEW THREATS

Once you've implemented some measures to minimize potential threats, it's a good idea to review all of them and to identify any new risks. If you've already been through the usual possibilities, try role-playing to work through the various possibilities, successes and failures.

Which analysis to use?

Are you having difficulty choosing which analytical technique to use for your particular decision-making situation? For each of the analyses described earlier in this section, this a list of common questions each analysis is most suited to answer.

GRID ANALYSIS

1 Do you have several possible options?

2 Are you finding it difficult to assess the implication of each option?

TRADEOFFS

1 Can you see the advantages of all the options but not the disadvantages?

2 Would you like to know how to discard some of the options?

PAIRED COMPARISON ANALYSIS

1 Are you having problems prioritizing?

2 Would you like to be able to compare options objectively?

DECISION TREE ANALYSIS

1 Would you like to have a better idea of the ultimate consequences of your decision?

2 Do you find yourself stuck in small details while failing to get a clear overall picture of your problem?

PLUS/MINUS/IMPLICATIONS

1 After much research, are you wondering whether it's actually better not to make any immediate changes?

2 Are you having doubts about the need for action?

COST–BENEFIT ANALYSIS

1 Do you have a clear idea of what course of action to take but are worrying about the total cost of the project?

2 Although everyone around you is talking about the benefits of the project, do you think they have overlooked expenses?

3 Would you like a way of calculating how much investment is needed and whether the benefits outweigh the expenditure?

PARETO ANALYSIS

1 Can you afford to make only one necessary change?

2 Would you like to know which of the changes will generate the greatest benefits?

RISK ANALYSIS

1 Are you afraid of changes and need some reassurance that your decision is not going to be a costly mistake?

2 Are you an optimist who finds it difficult to pick holes in ideas and would like a way of questioning why you feel so positive?

3 Are you committed to a project with an uncertain outcome and would like to find ways of minimizing the potential pitfalls?

Checklist: The alternatives

1 Have you listed your alternatives and included their respective advantages and disadvantages? ☐

2 Have you worked out all the possible consequences of the alternatives? ☐

3 Have you been able to prioritize both lists using the various techniques to put values on different options? ☐

4 What are the risks involved in the alternatives? ☐

5 How necessary is it to take the risk? ☐

6 Do the benefits of taking the risk outweigh the disadvantages? ☐

7 What will taking the risk accomplish? Are there any other alternatives for achieving your objectives? ☐

8 Have you determined the possible losses as well as gains? ☐

CHECKLIST

9 Have you listed all the positive effects of a successful outcome and all the negative consequences? ☐

10 Have you dismissed extremely remote or unrealistic possibilities? ☐

11 Do you have an accurate estimate of the probability of each case? ☐

12 Are you satisfied that this estimate is not based on your own personal approach to risk-taking? ☐

13 Are you taking too many risks at once? It's preferable to take one risk at a time.

☐

14 Is the risk–benefit ratio acceptable to you and to your company?

☐

15 What contingency plans do you have for the worst-case scenario?

☐

16 Could your company survive the worst consequence?

☐

CHECKLIST

Flaw: Ignoring corporate core values

However meticulously you follow a set of well-thought-out procedures to make a decision and analyze the facts of a problem, there is still an important element that steers most decisions. The subjective, intuitive feelings of the decision maker himself have a powerful impact on the process. Managers, like most people, are prone to overlook the role of their own personality in decision making. The main purpose of this section is to point out some of the common and often hidden obstacles to clear thinking caused by people's individual preferences, biases and habits.

Personal ambition and expectations certainly play a role in business decisions, but choices at work are not made in isolation from the surrounding environment. The decisions you make are unlikely to find support at work if they don't concur with the corporate culture. For instance, if the company is risk-averse, you will have to be less ambitious about the scope and speed of the bolder changes you would like to implement.

HOW TO OVERCOME THIS

1 Work with these boundaries firmly in mind. If you are working for a clothes retailer that has specialized in formal men's wear, it's going to be impossible to persuade them that the teen boys' sports sector presents the highest growth opportunity in the fashion sector. You might be better off trying to update the existing line of formal wear.

2 Become more savvy about identifying the attitudes and ways of working you value and comparing them with your targeted organizations. Find out if the company puts an onus on stability and experience ahead of innovation and modernization. Decisions are never taken in a vacuum. Any decision you make has to make allowances for the dominant politics and cultural values surrounding you.

Flaw: Letting first impressions rule

Tests show that an overwhelming number of people make decisions based on their first impressions. The same applies when people receive information. The first set of facts – which are often opinions couched as facts – are what will most determine the ensuing opinions and perceptions. Even during presentations, the first facts relayed by the speaker are regarded as the most influential in forming the audience's overall impression. Think how advertising in general aims for the pithy catchphrase or image that is intended to lodge in our brains before we can start analyzing more deeply the implications of the phrase.

HOW TO OVERCOME THIS

1 Ask questions, ask for explanations and don't take any fact or opinion for granted.

2 Seek information and opinions from a variety of people to widen your frame of reference. Don't dwell disproportionately on what you heard first.

3 Look at your own way of presenting facts to clients or colleagues when you are trying to impress on them your point of view.

Flaw: Taking refuge in the familiar

Apart from leaders, most people prefer not to rock the boat or challenge the status quo. There are several reasons for this, including laziness, the comfort of following what's been tried and tested and the fear of being exposed for an opinion or an action that challenges convention. Many businesses make a lot of money selling products and services that are popular mainly because they already have an established market and appeal.

HOW TO OVERCOME THIS

1 Always go back to your decision problem. How well is the familiar, established way of thinking serving your objectives?

2 Take a note of the many successful companies around you and remember what made them stand out in the first place. They probably offered an innovative product or service that was unfamiliar in the market and started a new trend.

3 Question why you are so desperate to conform and not to stand out from the crowd.

Flaw: The fog of personal preference

An executive of a car company may have a personal fascination with fast cars and allow this preference to guide his decision to invest heavily in the sports side of the market even though all the latest evidence might suggest that the family automobile represents the highest growth market in the next five years. This bias is a common flaw. People tend to persuade themselves of the correctness of a decision because they have a personal preference.

HOW TO OVERCOME THIS

1 Teach yourself to make counterarguments to your preferences or if you find this too difficult, get a colleague to play devil's advocate.

2 Force yourself to write down five reasons why the decision is the right one. By the third point, you will have gone beyond the personal hunches and will be forced to come up with hard facts.

3 Imagine you have to persuade people who have no interest at all in your product. They won't be able to understand your enthusiasm, let alone share it. They are only going to be impressed with numbers.

Flaw: Taking the frame for granted

The way a problem is presented to us tends to have a powerful influence on the way we perceive it and respond to it. For instance, one member of your company may ask you: 'Do you think it's a good time to be launching a product in Asia when so many of our competitors have tried that and they've faced numerous difficulties?' It's easy to take the question at face value and end up agreeing with the speaker because of the way the question was framed. The speaker could alternatively have presented the decision in a positive light: 'I wonder why some competitors failed to tap into the Asian market? Did they launch the wrong type of product? Was it the wrong time of the year? Have any companies in the sector succeeded?'

HOW TO OVERCOME THIS

1 When you are faced with a rhetorical or leading question, rephrase it or put it another way.

2 Look at a problem not as a problem but presented as potentially a hidden opportunity.

3 If you see the problem in an optimistic light, refrain from trying to influence others by presenting the question in a favourable light. Frame the question in a way that can't be answered by a 'yes' or 'no'.

Flaw: Justifying past decisions

People are often unwilling to free themselves from past decisions, even when they know deep down that these decisions did not achieve their intended objectives. Politicians are notorious for never admitting to mistakes (and it's often considered career suicide to do so), but business leaders, under the increasing glare of the media, are also prone to portraying themselves as infallible. Apart from what is perceived as public humiliation, admitting to mistakes might also incur the wrath of shareholders, senior bosses or personnel who suffered as a result of the decision.

HOW TO OVERCOME THIS

1 Look at every new problem in a fresh light and gather information on the possible alternatives without allowing a former decision (which might contradict some of the existing alternatives) to cloud your judgement.

2 Seek a relative newcomer in the company to bounce ideas off as he or she won't have any past associations or vested interests in past decisions.

3 Try to pinpoint exactly where you went wrong in the past decision. Maybe you've been exaggerating your own role in the process. Circumstances may have changed during the implementation that were beyond your control.

4 Look at the problem with a long-term view. How much will you lose by admitting to a past mistake compared to what you could lose by not righting it?

Flaw: Making unrealistic predictions

Opportunities can be anticipated and potential mishaps prevented by relying on educated estimates of future events. People, however, tend to fall into two different traps – taking an overoptimistic view of the future or playing it too safe. The two extreme cases are a result of basing future predictions on the memory of past events. People tend to remember the more dramatic stories – of people making a great fortune (hence being too positive about an outcome based on a desire to become rich) or of people losing everything (and therefore provoking a powerful fear of failure). In most cases, neither scenario plays out.

HOW TO OVERCOME THIS

1 If you can't forget the dramatic case studies initially, try to calculate how representative they are of their respective sectors. Look beyond the actual event and analyze the reasons for the huge success or whopping failure. Are there any indications that these same factors will repeat themselves in the problem you are working on?

2 Work toward a compromise. You don't need to work in extremes, if you have a tendency to be wildly optimistic, lower your projected figures by a reasonable percentage. If you are afraid about losing all your investments, just try making a small investment that won't unduly hurt you.

Flaw: Analysis or paralysis?

Managers are sometimes overcome by a fear of failure or an obsession for fact-finding that may prevent them from making any final decision. The tell-tale signs of this syndrome – commonly referred to as 'analysis paralysis' – are easy to spot. Managers, in an attempt to be taking positive action, make seemingly endless requests for more reports, studies, evaluations and statistics. Not happy with a pile of facts, they arrange meetings to discuss new findings and then demand even more information. Any decisions are literally paralyzed.

HOW TO OVERCOME THIS

1 Set a deadline for a decision and stick to it rigidly. Make sure you've announced the deadline to all the team with sufficient warning. By making the deadline public knowledge, you are not only forcing the team to work with urgency, but you are also forced to set an example. Only major external circumstances such as a sudden change in the market or an unexpected announcement by a competitor are valid reasons for postponing the deadline.

2 Don't be afraid to ask for help or seek advice from other senior managers. If fear of making the wrong decision is paralyzing you from making a decision, voice this concern with senior management or a client. They may agree with your point of view and encourage you to proceed. If their opinion varies widely, ask them to spell out what they think is wrong with your line of thinking. The best arrangement is to find a colleague in the team who can alert you to your tendency toward analysis paralysis.

Assessing your own style

Your decision making process can depend to a large extent on how you fit into the following areas, according to the well-known personality assessment tool, the Myers-Briggs Type Indicator (MBTI). Below is a description of each area and how it affects decision making:

THE EXTROVERT

How do you recognize one?
- Compiles information and develops ideas through interaction with others.
- Verbalizes ideas in order to reinforce them.

Effect on decision-making
- Likes to brainstorm ideas verbally.
- Thrives on making decisions in a group setting.
- Likes to react to others' comments and to receive feedback on his or her own ideas.
- Prefers face-to-face meetings to written communication (memos, e-mails and letters).

THE INTROVERT

How do you recognize one?
- Compiles information and builds on ideas in isolation and after much reflection.
- Keeps ideas and opinions to him- or herself.
- Prefers written communication to group meetings.

Effect on decision-making
- Before a meeting, prefers to work through all variables on his or her own, rather than rely on improvisation.
- Favours a period of reflection after listening to opposite or conflicting views.
- Likes to look over a completed written document describing the plan before making a final decision.

THE SENSER

How do you recognize one?
- Likes to focus on details.
- Learns through experience, rather than relying on theory.
- Can easily see the differences between two concepts.
- 'Knows' something because he or she has experienced it.

Effect on decision-making
- Looks for explicit evidence and past experience for analysis.
- Prefers to concentrate on operational issues.
- If data contradicts the prevailing theory, will rely on the data.

THE USER OF INTUITION

How do you recognize one?
- Prefers to look at things from a global perspective.
- Learns through applying theory, which can help make logical deductions.
- Can perceive the similarities between two concepts.
- 'Knows' something because it is a logical extension of a theory.

Effect on decision-making
- Likes to apply a model or theory to analysis.
- Once an overall strategy is agreed, will pay less attention to operational issues.
- When data conflicts with theory, will tend to go with the theory.

THE JUDGE

How do you recognize one?
- Likes to reach firm conclusions.
- Prefers order and structure.
- Pushes for a short information-gathering process.
- Thrives in ordered, regulated and controlled environments.
- Likes to finish one task before embarking on another. Is averse to multitasking.
- Plans activities thoroughly before starting

Effect on decision-making
- Pushes for definite closure.
- If other people present obstacles, he or she will do his or her best to remove them and stick with perceived winning formula.

THE USER OF PERCEPTION

How do you recognize one?
- Likes the process of information-gathering.
- Finds it difficult to stop researching and coming to a conclusion.
- Can move happily from one project to another.
- Prefers to avoid fixed plans and to keep options open.
- Likes thinking laterally.
- Is inventive and creative.

Effect on decision-making
- Finds it difficult to stick to a deadline.
- Will encourage group debate and will have no problem changing a decision if new information emerges.

THE THINKER

How do you recognize one?
- Uses logic in making decisions.
- Likes to use rationality and notices flawed reasoning in others.
- Uses an impersonal style that can be perceived by some as cold, hard or heartless.
- Can be thick-skinned.
- Is good at spotting tasks and goals to be met.

Effect on decision-making
- Can provide an objective and critical analysis.
- Can accept conflict as a natural, normal part of relationships with others.
- Operates from factual principles. Deduces and forms conclusions systematically.

THE FEELER

How do you recognize one?
- Uses personal feelings in making decisions.
- Is sensitive to others and will make sure other people aren't hurt.
- Takes things personally.
- Uses an empathetic style that can be misinterpreted as soft or weak.
- Thrives in a warm, friendly environment.
- Will use logic to serve their feelings.

Effect on decision-making
- Recognizes the feelings of others will lead to a decision based on consensus and harmony rather than on logic and dogma.
- May take longer to come to a decision because they are juggling other people's needs and reactions.
- May avoid making decisions that might be unpopular.

OVERALL CONCLUSION

While some people are fixed in their personality types and way of processing information, many others can display a range of these areas depending on their experience, age and situation.

Checklist: Factoring in the personal

1 Are you sure the decision isn't merely to further your own personal agenda? Have you taken into account the long-term objectives of the company in your decision? Is your proposal the most fitting for the type of company you work for? ☐

2 Can you remember the moment when you were first told about the main problem you are trying to resolve? What were your first impressions? Did they change once you found out more about the problem? ☐

3 Are you afraid that your decision will make you unpopular because it goes against the prevailing opinion? Is standing out from the crowd difficult for you? ☐

4 Have you made sure that your own personal taste or preference hasn't got in the way of your decision? ☐

4 Did you take the original framing of the problem for granted or did you try to look at it differently? Did you check that the original description accurately reflected the situation?

☐

5 Can you be certain that a past decision isn't influencing your decision now? Are you afraid to admit past mistakes? Can you see that admitting to mistakes now rather than later will save you and the company future problems?

☐

7 If you are naturally optimistic, are you sure that you've heard the points of view of a less positive team member? Similarly, if you tend to err on the side of caution, have you given some thought to enthusiasts within the team?

☐

8 Do you tend to postpone making a difficult decision? Do you have trusted colleagues who are prepared to give you a nudge when you look like stalling on taking further action?

☐

CHECKLIST

6

making and enacting
the decision

Checklist: A recap

The moment to make the final decision has arrived. If you work in a large company, you may still face the hurdle of having to persuade senior management that your decision is sound. But first, you have to convince yourself for the last time that you have made the appropriate option.

1
Go back to the very first step when you were deciding if there was a problem that needed solving. Can you describe the problem? Does it still require a resolution? Have you been exaggerating or minimizing the problem? If you've involved close colleagues in these final stages, it might be a good idea to ask a business friend at another company whether you've been inflating the problem. ☐

2
Have you lost sight of the company's main objectives? Are you sure this decision is addressing it or have you gone off on a tangent? Can you still answer the question 'Why is this important?' with conviction and persuade others the same thing? ☐

3 Have you thought about all the possible solutions and courses of action? Can you think of any other alternatives? Would your decision change if only you were given more information and time?

☐

4 Have you really considered all the possible outcomes of your alternatives? Was it an easy process to eliminate some of the potential solutions?

☐

5 Have you taken into account the company's corporate culture and the acceptability of your decision? Will it be difficult to persuade senior management that this is the appropriate course of action to follow?

☐

CHECKLIST

6 How risky is this decision? Have you been able to uncover all the possible eventualities? Are any of them dangerous? Have you looked at ways in which any negative repercussions could be minimized?

7 Would the decision change if you made it in two months' time? Will circumstances change considerably after that? If so, do you have contingency plans (in the eventuality that this decision isn't approved immediately and therefore not put into effect for another three months)?

8 Is it necessary to implement this decision now? How risky is it to delay this decision?

9 What would be the consequences of deciding to do nothing at all? ☐

10 Do you have the gut feeling that this is the correct decision? Are you happy with your option? ☐

11 Have you factored in all the psychological forces that block intelligent decisions? Are you in a calm enough state to make this sort of assessment? ☐

CHECKLIST

Last-minute doubts

Some of the obstacles caused by the decision maker's subjective, intuitive feelings were discussed on pages 164–179. Personal doubts and fears are bound to surface at the moment just before making the final choice and these are some tips to deal with these last-minute jitters:

1 TAKE THE LEAP OF FAITH
The fear of getting it wrong prevents many people from sticking their neck out on any decision. The burden of having to assume responsibility for a decision that may go wrong gets heaviest during crunch time.

Remember that all decisions are in the end a leap of faith, however many certainties you have bargained for. Think of the best-case scenario and what can be achieved as a result of the decision.

2 LIVE WITH IT
Accept the worse-case scenario, too – actually visualize it and analyze whether you could live with it. Would there be no way back? You may be overplaying your fear and forgetting the potential benefits of a successful outcome.

3 IMAGINE A DIFFERENT SCENARIO
What would happen if you didn't take this decision or if a senior director were to put a major obstacle in the way? Would you acquiesce or be sorely disappointed? There's nothing like the threat of something you've been working towards being taken away to test your resolve and commitment.

4 RECOMMIT

You may have spent so much time on the decision making process that you have lost sight of why you became involved in the situation in the first place.

Go back to the preliminary stage and remember what fired you up to tackle the problem.

Ask yourself if you are ready to commit to this decision and to take it to the next stage – to put it into action.

5 SEEK A SECOND OPINION
Pick a supportive business colleague (he or she doesn't have to be in the same company) and go through the case history of the problem.

You will feel buoyed by having an attentive listener who comes to the problem with fresh eyes. Make the most of the positive criticism and the encouragement.

6 ELIMINATE FEARS
Write down all your fears and then confront each one of them. Ask yourself what would be the worst that could happen if any or all of them came true?

making and enacting the decision

Seeking official approval

Whether you've been keeping colleagues and superiors up to speed during the process of your decision making or not, the time is still going to come when you have to make a presentation of some sort, either to a panel of executives or on a one-to-one basis.

The following are steps to follow to make the presentation process as smooth as possible:

1 FIND OUT PROCEDURES

You need to find out the company procedure for the official sanctioning of decisions and projects. Obviously a one-stop approval is going to be the easiest, but be ready to go through various stages in a company with a rigid hierarchical structure.

If you need several stages of approval, it's wise to spend some time courting the executives who must give a stamp of approval by briefing them in time and anticipating some of their questions.

2

PREPARE A REPORT
Even if you are required to make a presentation, it's imperative
to prepare a report to help crystallize your thoughts on paper
and for others to refer to after the meeting or at the various
stages of the decision making process.

Although you've been living and breathing the project, others
may only have a vague notion of the main issues, even if you
have kept them in the picture during the process.

3 WORK OUT THE IMPORTANT POINTS
The report should be as concise as possible and cover the following points:

- Why the decision was necessary in the first place
- What course of action to take
- Why this is likely to resolve the problem
- How long the action plan will take
- What will it involve
- How many people will be involved

4 MAKE THE PRESENTATION

Prepare the presentation with the same care and attention to detail and visual effect as if you were preparing a client presentation.

A coherent, confident speech will go a long way towards persuading others of your course of action before they've even started questioning the content. Be ready for the most demanding of questions so that you appear unfazed during the meeting.

5 PREPARE A SUMMARY REPORT

Even though you've performed well at the meeting, you may find it difficult to find out exactly how you fared, as some senior managers may take a few days to give you final approval. Sometimes, this is simply because they are attending to other business. To safeguard yourself, you can always prepare a final summary of the meeting itself, incorporating some of the questions raised and send it to the relevant decision makers to show you've taken any additional feedback or objections into account.

Deciding in a group

After a long period weighing decisions on your own, you may find it difficult to start compromising some details of your decision and the action plan, but you have to anticipate the need for a group discussion. These are three potential scenarios to look out for:

1 UNFOCUSED DISCUSSION
Although groups are sometimes better at solving problems than individuals on their own (the 'two heads are better than one' argument), group dynamics can also make joint agreements inefficient and unreasonable.

This is particularly the case if there are members in the group who are in competition with each other or who are using the meeting to further their interests rather than to focus on the decision at hand.

2 FOCUSED DISCUSSION
You have to make sure that you act as a cool mediator. Insist that the group follows an agenda; let them go through the pros and cons of the alternatives.

Encourage everyone to air their opinions. You want colleagues to leave feeling that a decision arose out of proper debate.

3 REJECTION

The unthinkable may happen. Your project idea is turned down by a majority at the meeting. Staying positive about your project doesn't mean you can't prepare yourself for the worst-case scenario – rejection of your proposal. It's useful to plan for the most negative consequence (as you may have done when you were calculating the potential risks of the project) so you know how best to react. Do you ask for a second consideration, ask for proper feedback or challenge the decision?

4 A VOTE

You may feel very vulnerable knowing that your weeks, possibly months, of work end up being decided by a show of hands. It's best to be prepared for this situation particularly when it looks impossible for the key executives to come to an agreement.

Remember that they are not deciding on you as a person but on whether a decision is appropriate for the particular problem. The upside of a vote is that you can gauge the exact level of support for the decision.

A go-ahead from just one senior manager still leaves you uncertain about the idea's acceptability further along the line.

5 NEGOTIATION

In the same way that you had to make swaps and tradeoffs when you assessed the alternatives so you can expect some horse-trading to go on among executives. Maybe there is general consensus with most of the elements of your decision but there are some sticking points.

If some members suggest making swaps, make sure these are appropriate and compare like with like. Ask yourself to what extent you are prepared to compromise, even though you may be constrained by the reality of what can be approved. Try to make all parties look like they've made gains by the end of the meeting.

Pitfalls to avoid

The period immediately following the final making of a decision is full of potential dangers and these are some common traps to avoid:

1 DOUBTING THE DECISION

Unless you are a seasoned decision-maker, it's natural to continue harbouring doubts even after making your final option. You can't gain from worrying or second-guessing at this stage.

No decision is ever set in stone. You can always go back and review it once you've given it the opportunity to create the desired outcome.

2 PREEMPTING VICTORY

You've spent so much time defining the problem, seeking a comprehensive list of alternatives, and deliberating over that final choice, that getting a stamp of approval can understandably feel as though you have jumped over the final hurdle.

The harsh reality is that if you don't take the implementation stage seriously, the first decision will only be an intention. You still have some way to go.

3 UNDERESTIMATING THE IMPLEMENTATION STAGE

No decision will be effective unless it's implemented properly. A real danger is that having finalized a decision, a manager loses interest in the project and expects the next stage to play itself out naturally. The success of the decision depends largely on how well you can enthuse a team to carry it out and how closely you monitor developments.

4 IGNORING OTHERS' UNCERTAINTIES

It's not easy to overlook the uncertainties of others, especially other staff members who haven't been living the decision process and have only been presented with the final decision plan. Try to remember the doubts and questions you went through at the beginning of the process and understand that colleagues may be wary of change.

5 FAILING TO EXPLAIN THE DECISION

Communicating the decision, its background, and how you came to make it is the next logical step to acknowledging others' uncertainties. Without persuading others of the importance of the decision, your chances of implementing the action plan effectively are severely minimized.

6 STICKING RIGIDLY TO YOUR OPTION
Naturally, you will be defending your fiercely fought-for
decision, but if you discover that there are unforeseeable
elements that are going to force you to make dramatic
changes once you've put it into action, don't fight it.

All managers make decisions that need reviewing, even
scrapping. Remember that the company's objective is
paramount. If the decision doesn't fit, then it's your
responsibility to find another one.

Setting a course of action

BUILDING A TEAM

Before announcing the decision to the entire company, it's useful to create an immediate team who are going to work closest with you on the action plan. There are several reasons for this:

1 You are going to need support to implement the plan, especially if there is opposition to the plan from some divisions. The more team members who understand and are able to sell your plan, the smoother the process will be.

2 Making an initial presentation of your decision to a small group of trusted team members is a way of testing all parts of the decision. The team may raise questions and point to consequences that you have overlooked. This is the time to iron out any flaws before the bigger company presentation that will follow.

3 You need help to implement the plan. You need to delegate and to make other key company members accountable to the plan.

4 You may need time to recruit new members if certain responsibilities can't be covered by your existing staff. Recruiting people takes time and money, and other departments will have to get involved.

WHAT IS THE BEST WAY TO DELEGATE?

1 CLARIFY ROLES
It's best to write down the main areas that will be affected by the decision. Is it the finance department? Are sales and marketing integral to the plan? Which divisions will be closely involved? Maybe you need more than two people looking after training?

2 MAKE INTERNAL APPOINTMENTS
Leave the final internal appointment until after the initial meeting so you know more about the reactions of colleagues to the decision.

You may be surprised by the input and enthusiasm of some members and decide that they will be able to manage a certain area better than someone you had earmarked earlier.

3 CONFIRM MISSION
Put any internal announcements in writing with a brief
description of duties and responsibilities. Invite team
members to get back to you with any queries.

4 BE OPEN TO SUGGESTIONS
The more input team members have on the project, the more
likely they are to be sold on the project and to maintain
enthusiasm and belief in the process.

Encourage ideas, not only because they may prove to be useful
but because they are a way of checking that members have
understood their briefs.

DEFINING THE PROJECT

These are key questions you have to answer before defining your project:

1 CLARIFY OBJECTIVES

- Can you describe in no more than two sentences what you want to achieve with the project?
- Do the other people involved understand the main objectives?
- Have you identified the constraints and limitations facing your project?
- What measures have you created to assess whether you have met your targets or not?

2 DECIDE ON TIME FRAME

- Have you estimated how long each activity or task within the project will take?
- Have you established an order for the activities?
- Is management or the client(s) imposing a particular deadline or do you have leeway in choosing the time frame?
- Once you draw up a time frame, have you accounted for any potential delays or obstacles? Do you have any contingency plans?

3 ESTABLISH A BUDGET
- Has management set out a specific budget or are you expected to come up with a budget and justify it?
- Have you calculated the costs for each key stage of the project?
- Have you set up a system to record all costs incurred as they happen?

4 MONITOR PERFORMANCE
- Have you considered how often you will need to use progress reports and review meetings?
- Have you set up an information centre where you and other team members can access project data and keep it up to date?
- Have you set up markers that will help you evaluate when your project has achieved its overall aims?

Announcing the decision

In a large company, inform a small group of trusted colleagues about a decision before communicating it to the majority of the workforce. Look at this as a trial run, or perhaps a safety net. It may also be safer politically. In smaller companies, a decision-maker may have to inform company members in one sitting or only after a preliminary meeting with one other colleague. In both scenarios, these are some guidelines to consider:

1 AVOID SECRECY

In the case of a large corporation, the least amount of time possible should pass between the first internal discussion of the decision and the communication to the rest of the company.

Leaks are often made, and rumours inevitably abound. It's advisable to suppress this period of speculation, which is damaging to morale, causes unnecessary anxiety, and can lead to the dissemination of wrong information.

2 TIME YOUR ANNOUNCEMENT

More often than not, the end of a week is the best time to make announcements because it causes less disruption to day-to-day operation. It also allows workers to digest the changes over a weekend break.

It's preferable to inform all departments at the same time to avoid the rumour mills. People also feel more united if they believe they hear an announcement at the same time.

3 AIM FOR FACE-TO-FACE
Although memos and, increasingly, email notices are the norm
for many announcements in today's workplace, it is still
preferable to make an announcement in person.

Obviously, in large offices, this poses logistical problems, but in
these cases, divisions could be informed in small clusters by
key members of the team.

People feel more closely involved in a face-to-face meeting.
They also feel less affronted by a potentially controversial
decision because a public meeting (of whatever size) provides
them with a platform to air their preoccupations and ask any
preliminary questions.

4 CLARIFY, EXPLAIN
Be precise in your announcement. Avoid the kind of corporate phrases that some companies use to cloak bad news. Make sure that the history of the decision and the company's key objectives are described in detail.

Approach this announcement as you would a sales pitch to a customer. You should try to present the decision in way that is sensitive to their needs.

5 INVITE PARTICIPATION
Be clear that you are open to suggestions and questions and that this announcement is not the final word on the decision plan, but the beginning of a strategy that requires all employees' involvement and input. If you've sold your decision well, you shouldn't feel threatened by this invitation.

making and enacting the decision

Making unpopular decisions

CHARACTERISTICS OF UNPOPULAR DECISIONS

1 When decisions are not perceived by subordinates as being a legitimate component of a manager's position, they are questioned or resisted. In short, they are unpopular.

2 The three areas that most commonly are met with resistance by workers are:
- Discipline
- Schedule changes
- Pay changes

3 Unpopular decisions are particularly disruptive in smaller companies with flat organizational structures and fewer levels separating the manager from employees.

STRATEGIES TO COUNTERACT RESISTANCE TO UNPOPULAR DECISIONS

1 EXPLAIN YOUR POSITION
In general, subordinates are most likely to comply with unpopular decisions if you are willing to take the time to explain the reasons behind the decisions. Just because you've been grappling with the decision for weeks, maybe months, don't assume employees have prior knowledge. You have to guide them carefully from the first steps, spelling out the original problem and the reasons why the decision will best resolve the problem and serve the company's interests.

2 ACKNOWLEDGE OTHER POSITIONS
It's a delicate balancing act to explain a decision that you have already made and to show others who are resisting the changes that you understand their concerns. Don't think that because you are allowing others to express opposing views that you are in danger of backtracking on your decision. However, there may be details in your decision that you may change as a result of employees' input.

Defending a decision

In an ideal world, the announcement of a decision is smoothly followed by a call for action. It's only natural that decisions, however necessary, are going to face opposition in a company. It's worth being prepared for objections.

The most confident managers will even see resistance as a positive part of the decision-making process because it challenges and tests the company's objectives. This doesn't mean the decision-maker is going to change the decision but he may fine-tune it to make it more attractive, not just internally, but for clients and suppliers.

1 ANTICIPATE DOUBTS
Many of the objections raised by either superiors, colleagues, or junior staff will have emerged during the decision-making process. These may even be the reason why it took so long to choose an option.

Make sure you've kept a record of the decision-making process, particularly the 'narrowing the options' stage, to see how you managed to persuade yourself or others that these objections could be overcome.

2 IDENTIFY DISSENT

Both during your preliminary presentation to a smaller team and later to a larger group of the workforce, there are ways to spot dissent. If a small group is gathered around a table, the person with his hand on chin could be showing scepticism, another person supporting his head with his hand is expressing doubt, while crossed arms reveal a defensive attitude. Frequent head nods and an open direct gaze will show support and appreciation but expect fewer of these positive messages in a preliminary meeting. Most people are cautious about their responses until they have fully digested the new information.

3 REMAIN CALM

When there is a growing chorus of disapproval, keep cool. You have anticipated doubts and you have to show that you are not caught unawares. Don't be hostile either. An aggressive stance only encourages an angry retaliation.

Show that you are willing to give them more time to thrash out objections. If there is no time in this preliminary meeting, either schedule a second meeting or arrange personal interviews if the number of dissenters is small.

4

RETHINK THE MESSAGE

If people fail to understand the reasons for your decision, it may be down to the way you've explained the decision. Have you assumed too much knowledge from the listeners? Have you forgotten to take them through the logical steps?

5

STAY OBJECTIVE

Look clearly at the nature and number of objections. How valid are they? Do they raise questions that are going to be made by the market and that you are unable to answer comprehensively?

Measuring progress

How do you anticipate the problems that are likely to arise during the implementation of a decision? No action plan is going to run perfectly smoothly, but these are some steps to ensure that you can minimize delays and, more seriously, prevent any major mishaps that prevent the desired outcome:

1 ESTABLISH BREAKPOINTS
The timing of a breakpoint will depend largely on the length of the action plan, but it is sensible in all cases to establish realistic intervals when key personnel can meet to exchange progress reports and views as to how the action plan is working.

2 STICK TO THE AGENDA

Few companies can stick faithfully to an agenda or template established in the early stages of an action plan because of the number of unforeseen eventualities. However, it is wise to establish a program with weekly or biweekly goals so that at breakpoint, staff can compare what has been achieved in practice with the idealized template.

This also allows you to ask specific questions about the progress report like 'What are the sales figures?' rather than 'So how are sales going?' which invites a vague reply. A template will also include details of budget and investment that can be quantified.

3 FOCUS ON ACTION
Although meetings are vital to air views and monitor progress, ensure that they end with a focus on generating further action with strict deadlines and targets that all key personnel are responsible for meeting.

4 COMMUNICATE PROGRESS
Whether things are going reasonably well or lagging behind schedule, it is important to keep members informed of progress so that they can measure their progress with other departments, for instance.

A positive update report can keep motivation going and show appreciation of hard work. Another report warning of potential problems ahead can alert staff in a clear way as to what is expected of them in the short term. Frequent communication also shows the decision-maker has a hands-on approach.

5 DOUBLE-CHECK PROGRESS
Don't rely solely on information gathered from meetings and memos. It's wise to make informal visits to different departments to develop a feel for how progress is going and to garner opinions from staff members who are not as involved in the more formal meetings.

6 REVIEW OBJECTIVES, ALTERNATIVES
The incessant questioning of 'what is important' that was necessary in the early stages of the decision-making process is equally valid at this stage. Halfway through an action plan, it is essential to review how much closer the company is to achieving what it really wants.

7 REVERSE DECISIONS
Hopefully, the underlying decision remains firmly in place but be prepared to make modifications to some of the subsidiary decisions that may not be achieving the desired results.

Checklist: Assessing the plan

An action plan doesn't usually have a neat cut-off point because objectives are constantly evolving. Most decisions that lead to a specific action plan are then superseded by another decision that is taken when a target has been achieved or circumstances demand the making of a new decision. It's useful, however, to try to stand back and understand why a decision worked or failed. These are some points to consider in making an evaluation:

1 Arrange a meeting with the initial group of people whom you entrusted to carry out the action plan. ☐

2 Encourage participants to provide feedback on what they think are the greatest achievements in the project and what were the biggest obstacles. Are there any areas that were less successful? What were the reasons for the problems? ☐

3 Make sure a member of the team is taking notes to provide a final report. This can be used by the company to refer to as part of the information-gathering stage of future decisions. ☐

4 Review the list of alternatives that the company could have followed before the final decision was made. Would one of the solutions have created a more positive result?

☐

5 Turn to the facts that can be quantified and compare whatever targets were initially set with what was in fact achieved.

☐

6 Ask participants to list more subjective achievements that were not necessarily part of the original action plan. For instance, customer service may have improved during the period as a result of greater staff motivation by the staff as a result of the general decision.

Or conversely, a certain part of the business has been negatively affected as an unforeseen consequence of the action plan. Does the value of the objective of the overall plan make up for negative side effects?

7 In the same way that it was necessary to communicate the original decision and the ensuring plan of action to the rest of the staff, the dissemination of a feedback report is also valid.

Assuming the decision has been mostly successfully, employees will benefit from feeling part of a positive experience. Even if there have been mishaps, employees can better understand why decisions were made and be more disposed to side with any decisions that must be made to improve the situation.

☐

CHECKLIST

Conclusion

This is a summary of the seven main stages that you will normally go through when making an important business decision:

1 DEFINE THE PROBLEM

It's imperative to describe exactly what your problem is so you can assess what decision you need to make. Coming up with at least two, preferably three, definitions of the problem is optimal because it will allow you to consider the greatest number of possible options.

2 SET OBJECTIVES

The next step is to formulate your company objectives. Can you see how resolving your problem will help to further the business's main objective? If so, you are on the right track. Now you can define your decision question along the lines of 'How do I make sure that the company's main objective is attained?'

3 IDENTIFY ALTERNATIVES

Your final decision will only be as good as the list of alternatives you come up with, so it's vital to spend time and effort gathering all the necessary research.

4
PROJECT OUTCOMES
To help you assess the validity of your different alternatives,
it's useful to analyze the potential consequences of each
option, using educated predictions.

5
NARROW THE OPTIONS
If you're finding it difficult to decide which of the predicted
outcomes most suits your company's needs, you need to make
lists of each option's advantages and disadvantages.

6
FACTOR IN THE PERSONAL
No decision is made completely in a business vacuum. Your
personal ambitions, objectives and tastes also play an
inevitable part in your decision. Challenge these.

7
IMPLEMENT THE DECISION
After months of consultation, the final approval might signal
the end of the decision-making process, but you have to make
sure the project is implemented.

Index